PRAYER
for everyday living

PRAYER
for everyday living

ALAN WALKER

Bounty
Books

First published in Great Britain in 2003
by Godsfield Press Ltd

This edition published 2005 by Bounty Books,
a division of Octopus Publishing Group Ltd
2-4 Heron Quays, London E14 4JP

Designed and produced for Godsfield Press by
The Bridgewater Book Company
Picture Research by Linda Marshall

ISBN 0 7537 1029 3
ISBN13 9780753710296

Printed and bound in China

contents

preface

As a child growing up in England in the 1960s, I was a member of what was probably the last generation to go to church out of social custom rather than because of my family's commitment. I wasn't brought up to "say my prayers" at home, but learned traditional prayers at church and as part of the daily act of worship at school. These often had beautiful words and, even if they did not immediately bring the world of the spirit to life for me, they certainly inspired me to search it out.

I always associate the beginning of my sense of prayer as more than words and as a genuine communication with the divine, with places in my neighborhood where—in the words of the poet T. S. Eliot—"prayer has been valid." Near my home, on a promontory surrounded on three sides by the sea, were the romantic ruins of a medieval monastery where for several hundred years the praise of God had been offered on a daily basis and the needs of the poor and sick of the area had met with great care and compassion. I found inspiration in wandering among the broken buildings of this holy place, and I did so for many years before I discovered that the life of their earlier inhabitants was not lost forever but was continuing in the hands of a modern community living only a few miles away. From my teenage years I became a regular guest of the brothers and sisters in their house, which also overlooked the sea, and during this time learned from them the monastic balance of work, study, and prayer, with every hour of the day devoted to its own special task and the whole consecrated to God in prayer.

When I was about sixteen another religious community established itself in our part of the country. A group of Tibetan Buddhist monks, forced into exile by the Chinese occupation of their country, settled in an old farmhouse and were grateful for the support of local people in helping them turn it into a monastery and meditation center. Despite the theological traditions that separated them from the Christianity of my upbringing, I immediately recognized the same spirit expressed in their life of teaching and devotion.

Since then I have explored many other religious traditions through study and sharing the lives of devotees. I have never found one that has not contributed something to my personal understanding of the spiritual journey. I hope that this book will be helpful to readers from all traditions and backgrounds, and that through it I will be able in some small way to express my gratitude for the blessings I have received from them.

Prayer is not a method or a technique, but a living, loving relationship, similar in many ways to our most important human relationships. I have avoided giving tips or recommendations about the best times, places, and postures for prayer in the belief that you the reader will discover what is best for you personally as you progress with this most natural of activities. I have suggested, based on my own experience and on the advice of many others far more qualified than myself, that you equip yourself with a notebook in which to record and treasure your experiences. What follows is taken largely from my own.

1: WHY PRAY?

What comes to mind when you think about prayer? Perhaps you were brought up to say your prayers before going to bed at night, to ask for God's blessing on your family and friends and for his blessing during the hours of darkness. You might have said a blessing before eating—a simple thanksgiving perhaps, or a special series of prayers and associated ceremonies before a meal celebrating a particular event in your tradition's calendar.

I went to a school where every day began with a hymn, a reading, and a prayer, and when there was some special occasion in our town to mark an anniversary or commemorate an event, it usually involved prayers and a religious ceremony.

However irreligious the modern Western world has become, we still turn to prayer to help us express our thoughts and feelings at the great moments in life such as the birth of a child, a marriage, or a death. We turn to prayer on an international scale to help us find our way after tragic or terrible events, such as those of September 11, 2001. And we find ourselves praying when we ourselves, or those we know or love, are in fear or in trouble.

So, most of us have some idea of what prayer is, and if we think about it for a moment we know there are several different sorts of prayer, even if we are not used to using special words such as *worship*, *thanksgiving*, *invocation*, and *petition* to describe them. We probably also have a sense that these things are not really what prayer is at its deepest. We have heard of meditation and contemplation and we know that in all the great religions of the world there have been people who have given up their whole lives to prayer, who have indeed turned their lives into prayer.

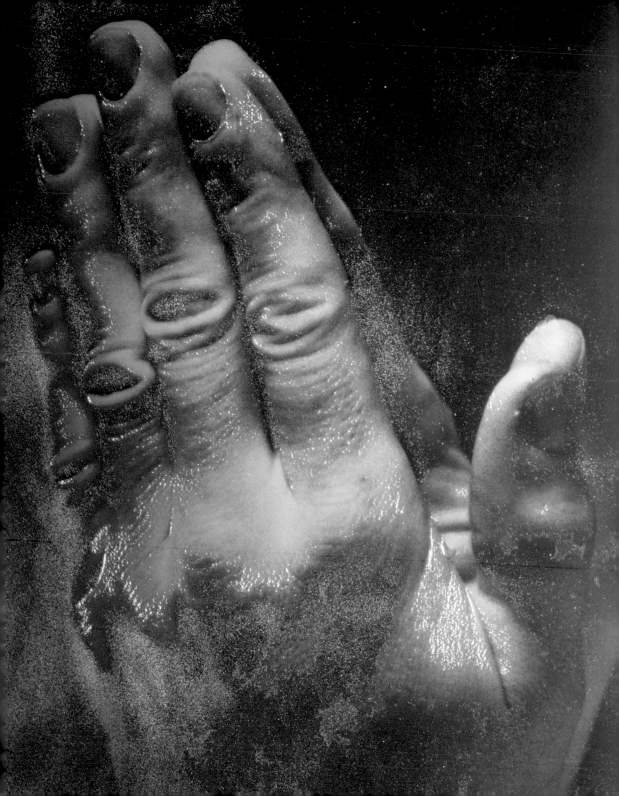

I believe that prayer is natural for human beings. Just as we need to eat and drink and breathe to stay alive, so I think we also need to pray to be fully alive. We are not just physical beings for whom survival and procreation is the only purpose. We are spiritual beings as well, with the capacity for a deeper relationship with the world and its inhabitants and with a destiny that stretches beyond our material existence.

I don't think it matters too much exactly what we believe at this point. Sometimes people think that in order to pray they need to have a full grasp of religious doctrines and the ability to compare religious traditions, and to come to some conclusion in favor of one of them. Some people get so caught up in teachings that they forget to put them into practice in their daily lives. But religions did not begin with all these doctrines and systems; they all began with very simple messages about how to follow the spiritual path. In other words, prayer came first, religion followed. All those labels—for different kinds of prayer, for example—are meant to be there to help us, not to make us worry that we are not knowledgeable enough to even begin.

Prayer came first. Our ancestors lived much closer to nature than we do today, closer too to their true nature. They had a sense of the sacred, indeed we could call it a knowledge of the sacred because they did not question the reality of the spiritual realm from which all things derived and to which everything was destined to return. Furthermore, however they would have expressed it, they knew that this realm was somehow greater and more dynamic than the material world. For instance, the spiritual world was not bound by the same rules of time and place as the material world. Our ancestors knew this because their ancestors who had died and entered the spiritual realm appeared to them in dreams and visions or sometimes as the shadowy manifestations we call ghosts. And when these dead ancestors appeared they could be again the children or young people they had once been; they could appear where they had never been; they could change the past.

Prayer was our ancestors' way of getting in touch with that other world. Certainly prayer involved speaking to the beings who lived beyond the material world and to that Being who seemed to lie behind the spiritual world and was responsible for its character and movement. But prayer was then much more than words. It could involve going to places where the material and spiritual worlds seemed particularly close and marking the visit with a special ceremony or ritual. It might mean spending time away from the usual activities of life to think about or reflect on the images that entered the mind when it was stilled. Or prayer could mean developing a kind of heightened awareness of the spiritual meaning or significance of everyday life and ordinary places and objects so that they could be read as messages from the spiritual world.

The world of our ancestors was an enchanted place, which we have made dull and mundane by thinking we can fully explain and account for everything, often using scientific archeological methods. Prayer is the way we can rediscover the lost world that lies hidden in front of our eyes.

It isn't really right to speak of spiritual and material worlds as if they were quite different from each other. Everything is spiritual and material—it's just that we don't see it that way. What we need to do is change our perspective on the world. At first we will get only hints and glimpses of the spiritual world that is all around us. Eventually we may come to live simultaneously in both the spiritual and material worlds. As the material body finally unwinds and eventually falls away in death, we hope that our spiritual selves will continue in a new existence where we will be reunited with our deceased friends and loved ones and with the Being we derive from. The people who have been called saints or masters in different religious traditions are those who have gone beyond glimpses of the spiritual nature of things to a more continuous gaze on the sublime, and who more particularly have sought to encourage others through their teaching and example.

But it is with glimpses and hints that we begin.

EXERCISE: MAKING WORD ASSOCIATIONS

Take some large sheets of blank paper and a pen—the type you can write with quickly and boldly. Perhaps you've attended a presentation where the leader has scribbled up the key points of a talk on a flip chart. That's the sort of thing we are going to do now. Just note down—in only a few simple words—everything that comes to mind when you think of the word prayer.

If you belong, or have belonged, to a religious tradition, or you have spent time studying religion, you'll probably start with lots of technical words, such as psalm *or* creed. *When you have filled a sheet with these words, pause and ask yourself how many of them someone from a different tradition—or without your education—would understand.*

If you do not have that religious background, you might find yourself struggling at first. That's because you think this is some kind of academic exercise since it involves pen and paper. Try just saying any words that come to mind out loud and then write them down. You'll probably think of terms such as ask, worry, God, pain, *and so on. Keep these words in front of you, because it's the people who have written down the technical words who need to start again on a fresh sheet of paper.*

The point of the exercise is twofold.

The first point is simply to free yourself up a little to start *considering* prayer. I like the word *consider* because it means so much more than to think about something in a detached way. Considering something means to give it your full attention, to show regard and care for it, to take it into account when you start to act. So when you *consider* prayer you are not just drawing on your knowledge and intellect, but on your memories and feelings as well. So, you should notice that when you think about prayer all sorts of emotions as well as ideas come to the surface.

The second point is to help you see that as you do the exercise you are actually praying. You are getting in touch with your spiritual side because you quickly realize that the very word *prayer* confronts you with what is most important in your life. You are praying already because you are focusing your thoughts and feelings on important issues; you are using your body to give these thoughts and feelings shape in the ceremony of putting pen to paper and then gazing at what you have created.

For people in the modern West there is probably no more appropriate and powerful way into prayer than through writing. Our culture has been formed and maintained by the written word. Writing is our most obvious route to self-expression. Whenever you want to pray but don't quite know how to begin, get some paper and start scribbling and then pause and *consider* what you have put down.

> *God needs to hollow us out, to empty us in order to make room for himself.*
>
> TEILHARD DE CHARDIN

To accompany this little book that I have written for you there is another greater book waiting to be written. This is the Book I suggest you write for yourself. I cannot tell you exactly what it will look like, but I hope you do not mind me making a few suggestions from my own experience and from that of others with whom I have tried to travel along the spiritual path.

Think of the book as *your* "Book." It's not really a journal or a diary, although you might want to date and locate the entries. It's not just a commonplace book, in which you write down quotations or examples of prayers you have come across. Call it *your* Book because you are writing it out of your own experience and considerations.

Use a blank book, such as a sketchbook, that has no lines on the pages. You'll find it easier to make the entries look attractive if you use a pen with a broad nib or a bold point. Leave big spaces between the entries and wide borders around them.

You already have some idea of how the book might take shape from the first exercise we did. You might want to copy the words you thought of then into your Book. For the most part the entries will be single words or short phrases that will be meaningful only for you.

Making entries in your Book involves three stages: First, pause to allow the words and images to surface into your conscious mind and then to settle themselves into some kind of order, with some moving into the foreground and others receding into the background. Second, write them down just as they present themselves and in the order that they do so. Third, return to your entries, perhaps soon after making them or possibly at some future time, to recover, mull over, and reflect on them in the act I have called *consideration*.

Treat your Book with care and respect, protecting it as you would a treasured family photograph album or letters from a loved one.

Because prayer takes you outside yourself, I would like to suggest that a good second exercise might be to bring to mind and record the names of individuals, living and dead, and issues that concern you and that you wish to pray about. Remember, as you do this you are already praying.

In the 1960s the English bishop John Robinson caused a sensation with his book *Honest to God*. The newspapers reported him as saying "Our image of God must go!" And some people started calling him an "unbelieving" bishop and much worse. Yet the bishop had certainly not said that he did not believe in God; he had just suggested that the image that most people have of God might be in need of some revision for modern times.

When we pray, who are we praying to? What image have we got of the being or beings who are the recipients of our prayers? What is the relationship between prayer and religion generally?

Some people would say that no one or nothing hears or listens to our prayers. When we pray, they contend, we are just giving expression to our deepest thoughts and concerns, but we are deluded if we think our prayers are going to make any difference to the world.

Others believe that anything is possible through the power of prayer, even miracles and extraordinary wonders.

To help us think through these questions we need to start with our image of God. I am assuming that most readers of this book have been brought up within the monotheistic (one god) tradition of the "Abrahmaic" religions of Judaism, Christianity, or Islam, and if not within this tradition then in a context where religious vocabulary and images are monotheistic. By this I mean that most readers are probably familiar with the religious belief in one God who made and upholds the universe, who has a

personal character and who is concerned for the well-being of humanity. As long as we do not give a name to this God, this picture of religion would probably also be recognizable by people from many other faith traditions of the world as well.

This picture of religion may be recognizable, but it is not really adequate. The definition of religion given above is most likely to be given by someone who does not actually believe in God. For instance, the idea that there is a creator and sustainer of the universe is something that I do not personally believe. People who are religious, who do believe, all have their own images and ideas of God. I am talking now about the way people differ, not the way religions differ. Each and every one of us has our own image of God.

Pause for a moment and ask yourself what your God looks like. You probably hardly need to pause because I suspect that, as you have been reading these words, your own image has been pushing itself to the front of your mind. Who is God for you? What is God for you? Perhaps you have a picture of God as a wise old man or woman, as a serene, sagelike figure resembling a Buddha image, or maybe you do not see God as a person at all but as a sense of power, like nature itself. These examples are only ideas, and it may be that when you think of God, it is feelings that come to the forefront: comfort or relief, anger or bitterness.

You could almost say that, whether God exists or not, he invokes powerful feelings in us, so those people have a point when they say that in prayer we are just giving expression to our deepest thoughts and concerns. Those people might also be prepared to agree that in the light of our modern "science" of psychotherapy—the "talking cure"—the act of expression itself is likely to bring about change. In this way, even the prayer of the unbeliever might be effective in helping such a person get to know and change himself or herself!

I am assuming that most readers of this book in fact have some belief, even if they cannot or would not wish to identify with a definite religious tradition. But I think we have to be careful not to confuse official dogmas with our private beliefs. We should accept that private prayer might be powerful enough to bring about that greatest of miracles—personal change.

It is helpful as we begin to pray to reflect on our own faith journey up until this moment, to try to get a sense of who we are and what God means to us.

EXERCISE: GETTING TO KNOW YOURSELF

• *In your Book write down the words that come to mind as you look back over your life. Don't try to be systematic or aim for completeness. Just jot down the words as they come to mind. Aim for about a dozen entries. Many of these words are likely to be names: of people or of places that have been important for you. This simple exercise can be quite powerful, even disturbing emotionally, because we may feel it is a kind of audit of our achievements and failures. Try not to get too drawn into the feelings evoked. What you are trying to do is to get to know yourself a little better, not to judge yourself. Think of the exercise as a prayer, a prayer for understanding, tolerance, and strength. Stand outside of yourself as an observer. Learn about yourself as if you were someone else who is caring for you and is concerned for your needs.*

• *On another occasion sketch out your story more systematically. Start somewhere toward the middle of the page with your place and date of birth, leaving space for the same details of your parents and grandparents, brothers, and sisters. Continue with your schooling and work experience, the places you have lived in and visited. Write down some words that express your character and personality and draw in some lines linking these words with the family members with whom you share them or from whom you have inherited them. Don't worry if the page gets messy and complicated—your life itself is rich and complex.*

• *Pause again when you have finished. Think about this exercise and the previous one, each in the light of the other. Try to see and accept how your own self-perception might depend as much on your background and opportunities as on your personal decisions and efforts. Remember, you are not trying to prove or explain anything; you are just trying to get a sense of how everything fits together for you. The aspects of your life combine in a unique way, but one in which so many other people are involved.*

EXERCISE: MAKING A FAITH DOSSIER

Jot down the outlines of your religious biography. Start with the external version: circumcision, baptism, confirmation, bar or bat mitzvah, attendance at church, mosque, or temple; any outward form of religion in which you participated by choice or convention. Then try a more internal version: a record of moments when you felt moved or touched by something outside of yourself that you feel might have been spiritual in any sense of the word. Did these personal experiences correspond to any of the official religious moments?

These exercises often bring up powerful feelings, and you may want to spread them out over a few days or more. Using the Book to discover and record the experiences can help us deal with some of these feelings. It can also be helpful to share them with a trusted friend who you know will be sympathetic to your desire to discover and grow in prayer.

If there is a single word that sums up the object of these exercises it would be *freedom*. Reviewing your life shows how much of who and what you are is the result of circumstances beyond your control, but it also reveals the power you have to strike out in new and unexpected directions. Even with a complete knowledge of your background, no one could ever have actually predicted how you would be. Furthermore, no one is able to determine even remotely how the future is going to be for you. Now that you know so much about your past, try to accept it and move forward into a future that is full of possibilities.

You have discovered too that the external moments of religion do not particularly correspond to the internal moments of faith. The space that lies between religion and faith is also a place of freedom. You need neither reject nor be bound by official images of God. These images exist to help you discover your own ways of thinking about something that, after all, cannot be pictured in human terms. And there is no need to turn your personal beliefs into dogmas that impede your freedom to reinvent and reimagine them in the future.

Everyone is free to discover prayer for themselves, and to pray in their own way. However, I would suggest that if you do belong to a particular tradition, either actively or only because of your family background, you begin your spiritual exploration within that tradition rather than assume that there is something greater or better to be found elsewhere. So many who have made the spiritual journey have echoed the words of the poet T. S. Eliot, who said that the conclusion of our exploration is to find ourselves at home again and to know the place for the first time. There is much to be learned from other faiths, and the more we get to know and understand each other's beliefs, the better, but a critical and balanced acceptance of our own past, and that of our parents and home culture, will provide the firmest foundation for spiritual growth.

Prayer is the raising of the heart to God.
God is greater than the creeds.
God said, "I was a hidden treasure and I wanted to be known, so I made the world that I might be known."

MUSLIM HADITH

3: expressing your devotion

Worship lies at the heart of religion and yet it seems strangely alien to us today. Prayer on behalf of others expresses our concern and generosity. We think contemplative prayer may be beneficial to our mental health in reducing stress and helping us relax. But devotion, the prayer of adoration, praising God for being what he is, appears somewhat primitive. It seems to suggest that God needs our flattery or that we fear he will turn against us if we fail to praise him and might retaliate by forestalling the sunrise tomorrow.

We might be reluctant to worship God, but there are plenty of other things we are happy to venerate. It may not be coincidental that the less room the modern world has for God, the more it seems to look for substitutes among the ranks of sports and entertainment celebrities. Revealingly, we often call such people "idols."

The Jewish and Christian traditions are radically opposed to the worship of idols, hence the commandment against making graven images of God. At the simplest level the traditions oppose the making of false images, but more profoundly they challenge the human impulse to worship money, power, gold or precious jewels, beauty, or some other mundane reality.

Worship is the primary form of prayer because it expresses our very deepest values. Are we turned toward God or are we bowed toward something in the world? Are we searching for the holy, or for something that brings us fleeting satisfaction and makes us the envy of others?

EXERCISE: ANALYZING WORSHIP

In your Book make a quick list of who and what comes to mind when you think of the word worship. *You don't need to think of what you worship, just how the word is popularly used in the media and in conversation.*

Read through your list. The word idolize *could probably be substituted in every case. Think about these objects of worship. What would be their attitude toward people who worship them? Do money and power care for those who possess them? Do movie stars have deep feelings for their fans?*

Recognizing our contemporary tendency toward idolatry helps us to see why worship seems alien to us today. Our fantasy is that it is only worth worshiping something we think we might ourselves become, at least in part: rich, powerful, beautiful. However, the true object of worship challenges the value of these things and indeed of all that the world holds in esteem. It demands reverence precisely because it is "wholly other" and beyond our grasp, and it does not promise any earthly reward in exchange.

Why then worship? Because we perceive, however dimly at first, that this God who is so different from us, so completely remote from anything we can conceive or understand, also lies at the very depth of our being—he is closer to us than we are to ourselves. It is through worshiping him that we can grasp how this can be so. Worship is not the uttering of words of flattery, but an attempt to transfer all of our feelings of value from the trivial to the sublime. It is a kind of self-emptying—not surprisingly often expressed in music, song, and dance—a losing of ourselves that exposes the divine within us.

True worship is also a response. You can address God because God has already spoken to you and you have heard the divine word. There is so much noise in the modern world that it's hard to listen. Your senses are bombarded with so much stimulation from the media, from advertising, from competing businesses that silence feels strange, as if something is missing. You may have become fearful of silence because it confronts you with the true character of existence. If I am not distracted by the noise of the world, I have to recognize and accept who I am. If my mind and senses are not carried away to some fantasy realm, I am forced to be here in the present, the place where hope and reality meet.

EXERCISE: SEEKING OUT SILENCE

• *Think about your day. In your mind run through its pattern from morning until night, from the time you get up, through your journey to and time at work or doing the domestic chores, your meals, your meetings, your time of relaxation. Go through it again and try to recall the sounds that accompanied each activity: the radio or television, the conversation and background music of shops and offices. Were there any moments of silence in the day? How did you feel during them? In modern urban life such times tend to belong to "in-between" moments, such as when you are waiting for an interview or meeting, for a delayed train or late appointment. Silent times are anxious times.*

• *Try now to give yourself some silence. Find a quiet place where you will not be distracted and sit comfortably for five or ten minutes. Don't choose a time when you are tired and need rest. Try to make time for this exercise in the middle of a busy period. Just sit and try to be aware of the noise in your head as all the concerns of the day rush through. Just let them run past your inner sight so that you can see what they are without becoming attached to any one in particular. After a while ask yourself where you are in all this activity. Imagine yourself in a busy street of a city you do not know and where the signs and notices are written in an alphabet you cannot read. Now think of yourself sitting quietly at home in your room in the evening. Just observe the contrast between the busyness and stillness of the two scenes.*

• *On another occasion seek out a place of quiet, in a park for instance, and give yourself a longer time, perhaps up to an hour. Although you have chosen this place for its quiet, notice how many sounds there are: the singing of birds, the sound of the wind in the trees, the distant hum of traffic. Give some attention to each one before moving on to another. How many sources of sound are there? But now listen more deeply with your inner ear. Think of yourself as being addressed by these sounds. They are calling to you, the birds and the wind, your fellow humans beings going about their lives. They are asking for your attention. They are there for you. Try to be with them as you might sit quietly with a loved one.*

Through exercises and experiences such as these we come to realize that silence need not be frightening. But more than that we begin to get a sense of our existence itself as a kind of response to something we hear in the silence. All the great religious traditions agree that when we come finally to stand before the divine, the only possible response we can make is silence—awed silence—the silence of worship. "Be still and know that I am God," the Hebrew scriptures teach.

But it is not silence that lies at the heart of the universe. We do not worship silence. We worship a divine reality that is not turned inward on itself but outward toward us, toward you and me, that elicits a response from us rather than being something we observe in a detached way. In the religions that emerged in the Middle East, this reality has been presented as a personal God speaking to us; in Christianity in particular "the Word was in the beginning with God and the Word was God" (*St. John's Gospel*). In the Indian tradition the divine emanates the sacred sound OM, which is beyond words and is itself the One, the ultimate. "One should know OM to be God seated in the hearts of all" (*Mandukya Upanishad*).

You do not need to worry too much about the theology behind these ideas. You are not engaged in an academic exercise but are on a spiritual quest. What you need to grasp is not some understanding of the nature of God (as if any of us could ever know that), but a sense of yourself as addressed by God. The sacred word is always being spoken to you and because there is nothing you can say that is going to add in any way to God, your response must be one of awe, of worship.

If you are going to pray you must begin with worship because it is worship that makes prayer, not meditation or some kind of therapy. Prayer is, before anything else, the human response to the divine reality, which must be one of awe and reverence. Think of standing for the first time before a tremendous mountain range such as the Himalayas. Words fail you in the face of such stupendous power and beauty. You do not need to congratulate God for being God any more than you would congratulate

the mountains for being big. God does not depend on our worship, but we depend on God and so worship can be defined as both the glorification of God and the sanctification of all that is human.

Worship is a process rather than an event. Once you have heard God speaking to you, you want to go on listening because you appreciate that you are transformed by the divine word. You start by setting aside special periods taken out of your daily life, but you know that these odd moments of particular attention are calling you to an ever deeper response. The early Christian monks sought to obey the scriptural call to "pray without ceasing" by developing an attitude of constant devotion. Every activity of life became for them an opportunity to praise God, because everything was seen in the light of its divine origins and purpose.

However, we are not monks, and given all our domestic and work responsibilities, we might be wondering whether we have any time for prayer at all. The way forward is to think in terms of regular rather than lengthy periods of prayer.

Perhaps you have an elderly relative or neighbor you visit. You'll have probably realized that frequent short visits are better than long occasional ones. Every ten-minute visit gives your friend something to look forward to and prepare for, something to occupy his or her thoughts and hands. Each one provides him or her with the opportunity to give you hospitality and to receive your appreciation and thanks. But the visits themselves are short and therefore not exhausting. They are occupied with the ritual of entertainment, however simple: decoration, refreshments, and so on. You do not arrive with a heavy heart because it is so long since your last visit and you are wondering how you will fill an hour of conversation. Instead of having to play the good neighbor, you have allowed yourself to become a welcome guest, a receiver rather than a giver.

Worship can be something like that. Aim for short but regular periods of prayer. Create rituals to express the specialness of the period, but leave time for silence. This book is not intended to be a manual and I do not want to impose on you ways of

praying that may not suit you, but I would emphasize the need to set aside a period each day for your prayer. The very idea of setting a time aside reminds us that prayer is more than just emergency communication. It is something we need to do because of what we are. The prayer period is like a meal for the spirit, essential for its well-being but also an occasion for creativity and a degree of formality. We live in an informal age but we still understand that formality is a part of any celebration.

Think of your prayer time as a celebration for God. The time you have chosen is the time on the invitation. Would you not bother turning up to a wedding or put off your appearance until the next day? Your attention is directed to God as it would be to your host or to those in whose honor the party is being held. The nature of the event dictates so many details of your behavior, from how you dress to your thoughts.

Identify a time for prayer, when you can put aside 20 minutes for God. Make it a time when you are not going to be exhausted or overwhelmed by thoughts of the things you need to do afterward. Find an appropriate place for prayer, if possible somewhere other than where you spend most of your time, somewhere quiet and without distractions. You might want to mark the place with a picture or an image of some kind, if you belong to a religious tradition. A flower or an attractive stone will help link the place in your mind with the world outside. Place or touch the object you have selected to mark the beginning and end of your prayer period, and your removal from and return to ordinary time.

Prayer should always begin with worship, the calling to mind of the divine in acknowledgment and gratitude for our lives. Since you are starting out in prayer you might want to prepare for worship by jotting down in your Book short lists of people and events in your life for whom to offer special thanks. You can then read reflectively through these during the prayer period, saying the words out loud if you are comfortable doing so. Do not let any activity of this kind fill or dominate the period. Remind yourself what prayer is, using a phrase you have composed or a quotation that has particularly struck you: something such as "Prayer is the opening of my heart to God." Recall that prayer is listening to God, putting yourself at the disposal of the divine, and then do this in several minutes of silence.

Don't rush suddenly away from prayer. At a party you make your farewells and offer thanks; you make arrangements for another meeting and pass on best wishes to mutual but absent friends. Do the same in prayer. Walk down the path knowing you have rounded things off properly for you and for your host.

Just as you might record a party, especially a special one, in your diary by keeping a list of people you met and what you discussed and did, so use your Book to do this for your prayer period. Only a few words are necessary: what kind of prayer you engaged in, what came to mind, what feelings you experienced. If you prayed in the morning glance at your Book in the evening; similarly if you prayed at night try to find a moment to look at it in the morning. Only a minute or so is needed for this review, but it will help you see your whole day as being framed with prayer and worship.

Devotion

I breathe, I speak, I praise You Lord.
Father God, Mother God be my
Brother God, Sister God.
I pray to the Glorious, He is
enough for me.

AFRICAN PRAYER

4: asking for help

Asking for things is probably what comes into most people's minds when they hear the word *prayer*. The word *prayer* originally meant "to plead" and for many today prayer is still a kind of last resort, a desperate turning to God for help because none is available elsewhere.

You have probably at some time in your life found yourself calling out to God for help to get you through a terrible moment. As likely as not, you made some kind of promise at the time that if you did find a way through this difficult or unpleasant situation, you would make changes in your life and do all sorts of things for God and other people in return.

Have you ever been or felt you were in real danger? You'd probably rather not remember what it was like—the feeling it created in the pit of your stomach and the other bodily reactions. What went through your mind at the time? Who did you think about? If you have been lucky enough to avoid such an experience yourself you may know the anxiety of waiting for news about a loved one who has been in the operating room or who has gone missing. What about as a child? Can you remember waking in the dark and feeling alone, crying out and no one coming? All of us, I am sure, have had moments when we have called out to God as the only one who can help us.

I don't want to make you dwell on painful memories, but thinking about times when you have been afraid and have looked to God for help is one way of remembering how dependent we all are upon him. It's easy to think about God when we are feeling desperate; it's much harder to do so when life is going our way. In the same way, one of the hardest things for us to understand about God is that he is not just the answer to big questions, such as the meaning of life and the origin of the universe; he is also the one who makes sense of everything we know and already experience.

The world makes sense to God, but it doesn't always make sense to us. One of the main objections made to religious belief is that God seems to allow bad things to happen and evil people to prosper. Furthermore, prayer for what is obviously just seems not to be answered. On the other hand, most people would agree that things often turn out in very unexpected ways and what looks at the time like a bad turn of affairs actually made possible all sorts of positive developments. This can even be said of terrible events on a grand scale, such as those of September 11, as well as of the many personal tragedies and disappointments we suffer.

Spiritual progress is often compared to training for sport. Every athlete and sportsperson expects to lose at least now and then. If they didn't they would have little incentive to improve their performance and victory would have little meaning. When spiritual writers talk about exercises, people unfortunately tend to hear only their emphasis on the need for practice and perseverance and then start to feel bad for missing a prayer time or neglecting to do some special reading.

It's obvious that an athlete needs to keep himself or herself in shape, but training involves more than that—it includes competition with your own past timings and achievements, and especially, real and practice trials against others. And this involves defeat. There may be scholars who have never known anything other than A grades, but there can be few sportspeople who have never lost a competition. Academic brilliance often seems to be effortless, while sporting prowess is a far more complex gift depending on a great combination of factors and opportunities, and one in which achievement is always based on overcoming the realities of past disappointment and of certain future decline.

I am comparing the spiritual and sporting lives because both involve appreciating and accepting that not only do strength and progress come from setback and defeat, they even depend upon them. The athlete does not give up on losing a competition, but becomes inspired and determined to do better. The spiritual person does not declare the world meaningless and without purpose because horrible as well as beautiful things happen.

You could say that whenever you pray for someone or for something to happen in a particular way, you are praying for the strength to accept that the world makes sense to God, and to have some insight into God's purpose for the world. Accepting that God has a purpose for the world helps us deal with the difficult question about *intercession*, as this kind of prayer is called—if God knows what is going to happen, and everything that happens is according to God's will, what is the point of asking? Surely all that you can do is accept what happens with an attitude of devotion and resignation?

The fact that God knows what is going to happen does not take away our need to make decisions. God might know what the weather is going to be like today, but I still have to choose what to wear. If I put on a raincoat or carry an umbrella I am hardly thwarting his plan that I should get wet and catch a cold! Rather than saying that God knows everything that is going to happen, which sounds as if everything has the same importance or significance, maybe it would be better to say that God cannot be surprised.

Praying for someone is like making a decision to help them change for the better. If someone is sick, for example, you might pray to help them get well again or suffer less. You can't always do anything material to help that person because you don't have the necessary skills or knowledge, or because you are simply too far away. When you pray for someone you are aligning yourself with God's will for that person, which will always be in his or her best interests, for God would never wish anyone harm. When we say that all that happens does so according to God's will, I think we might be turning God into a bit too much of a tyrant. Wouldn't it be better to say that what God wants is that the world should discover that its own best interests coincide with his intentions for it? God wants us to realize this for ourselves and choose to live our lives accordingly, rather than just obey him because he is the boss!

When you see that people are in need your reaction should be to try to help them as best you can in every way you can. This itself is prayer because you hope you are doing what is best for them. The less you are able to help, the more your prayer turns into words, but it is your desire and decision to help more than the words themselves that form the true prayer.

We cannot surprise God but God can surprise us, and usually does. Prayer is always an encounter with a mystery, so our desire to cooperate with God through helping others must leave room for an acceptance that what we imagine to be for the best may turn out to be misconceived. We need to learn that, even if what we pray for does not come to pass, our deeper prayer that God's will be done has not been rejected.

May we become at all times,
both now and forever,
a protector for those without
protection, a guide for those
who have lost their way, a ship
for those with oceans to cross,
a bridge for those with rivers
to cross, a sanctuary for those
in danger, a lamp for those
in need of light, a place of
refuge for those in need of
shelter, and a servant to all
those in need.
THE DALAI LAMA

Sometimes even books about spirituality give the impression that praying for others is not very important or is a lower form of prayer. This is quite wrong. It is an immensely important kind of prayer, which needs to be done right if all prayer is to be done right. The mind and the heart cannot rise to God in prayer without paying attention to what is happening in the world.

You are not alone in the world and you cannot abandon your responsibilities toward your family and your community with the claim that you are following a *spiritual* path. God's plan is for the world, not just for you. What is truly best for each of us is to cooperate with God's intentions, and action and prayer for others is the clearest expression of our determination to do this.

Who should you pray for? You should pray for everyone because you want God's will to be achieved, but it is hard to feel personally involved with everyone and so your prayer runs the risk of becoming little more than a vague hope that everything will work out for the best. And for your prayer to be truly prayer you need to be personally involved and ready to take the risk that you yourself might have to change in order for God's project to be put into effect.

EXERCISE: PRAYING FOR OTHERS

• *First of all you should pray for yourself, so that you become an instrument of God's will in the world and have the strength to accept the challenges that this could bring.*

• *Then think of the circles of those close to you: your family, friends, work colleagues, acquaintances, and then move beyond to your neighborhood and community. Just letting your thoughts move through these circles will probably bring to your attention some faces and names of people who are in need of prayer, for whatever reason. Some might be sick or bereaved or facing difficult circumstances, others might be at turning points in their lives, such as marriage or childbirth. When you have identified them you may want to write their names down in your Book or elsewhere so that you can bring them before God in prayer.*

• *You already began to pray for others when you brought them into your mind as people in need, but you will probably want to focus a little more on expressing your wish to help them. Write the names of these individuals on separate pieces of paper or on file cards so that you can concentrate on each one individually during prayer. The card represents the person and should be treated reverently, being taken up and laid down gently in a prayerful context, as you would a sacred image or holy text. If you have a regular prayer time you could pray for particular groups on particular days.*

• *This kind of prayer should always be accompanied by some consideration of practical ways in which the subjects of your prayer can be helped. Praying for the poor, for example, would be a little strange if you did not also make some small financial contribution to relieving poverty. You might not have the skills or qualifications to help the sick, but a gesture such as a visit or a letter to a sick person is usually greatly appreciated and might even relieve some of their pain and depression. When there is nothing practical that you can do or you need for whatever reason to remain anonymous, a symbolic expression such as lighting a candle or making an offering to charity will help you engage more fully with the working out of God's purposes.*

PRAYER FOR THE DEAD

A special group for whom you might feel called to pray is the dead. Religious traditions differ on whether the eternal fate of the individual is fixed at death and the departed are "beyond" prayer, but it is undeniable that the wish to pray for the dead is strong. The dead are beyond our help in every other way, and so often we have lost them before we have been able to fulfill our relationships with them.

In the West today, death is often treated as a sign of failure or as something almost unnatural. People are very reluctant to talk about death, and funerals are sometimes hastily organized, even embarrassing occasions. In traditional societies, on the other hand, the celebration of death was an important moment in the life of the family and community. The ceremonies associated with death were believed to help the progress of the deceased person to the next stage of existence and also to assist the bereaved in coming to terms with their loss. Modern people often die invisible deaths in hospitals, sometimes without the knowledge of neighbors or anyone but the most immediate family members. Not surprisingly, people who have lost a loved one find it difficult to adjust, since the world has not noticed or taken account of the pain that often haunts them for a long time.

Prayer for the dead certainly has a value in helping those who remain come to terms with their loss. The form of such prayer can be similar to other prayers of petition, such as the writing down of the name and the holding up of a photograph of the deceased. Prayer for the dead is particularly appropriate on the anniversary of the death, when a visit could be made to the grave or the place where the ashes were scattered or the funeral took place. Symbolic or ritual expressions of grief and well-wishing, such as the placing of flowers or a stone, can stand in for the words that cannot express the sense of loss and the feelings that are brought up.

5: asking for protection

I was brought up in what had once been a fishing village. A century before I was born it had also been an artists' colony, attracting painters who were charmed by what they saw as the picturesque life of the fisherfolk. Their paintings picture the men going out to sea in open row boats or dragging their boats back onto the beach after many hours on the high sea. They show the women working on the nets or packing the fish into baskets, which they would carry on their backs to market. But they also frequently portray another scene, that of the women, the wives, mothers, and daughters of the fishermen, just gazing out to sea as a storm brews and the sky grows dark. They are fearful for the safety of their men at the mercy of the cruel sea and the weather. Most of them no doubt will have had prayers on their lips.

In our modern lives we face all kinds of dangers, but they are very different from the ones that confronted our ancestors. They lived much closer to nature and the elements. The sea, the wind, and the earth could be friends or enemies. Nature was to them both awe-inspiring and frightening. They came to believe that these powerful forces that had such a tremendous influence on their lives were expressions of divine activity. The gods favored them with a calm sea or showed their anger with a storm.

People were moved to worship and devotion because they perceived their lives and all that they had as gifts from God. But they came to realize also that their relationship with God resembled human relationships. The feelings they had toward God were like those they had for other people. They had a profound respect and gratitude for God the parent, together with a sense of dependency and responsibility to fulfill challenging expectations that they might not have chosen for themselves. They had a deep sense of attraction toward God the loved one, who was both appealing and mysterious and who seemed at some times to want nothing but their happiness, and at others to need their total attention. God was not simply there. He was there to be known, to be known as one would another individual, and who—like other people—could never be fully known.

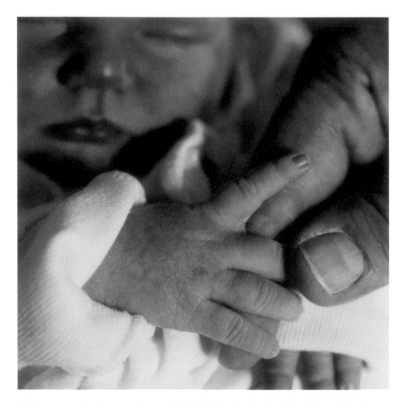

Religious people often use the word *faith* to describe their relationship with God.
To the modern ear this sometimes sounds like a kind of vague belief, an inferior sort
of knowledge, a "not quite sure but I hope it's true" attitude. But *faith* really means
"trust or confidence in someone you already know or have started to get to know."
Our relationship with someone may have its ups and downs yet still deep down
be one of trust. I think we could go further and say that in nearly all human
relationships what we are trying to establish is trust. We might use different words to
describe romantic encounters, business partnerships, and ordinary acquaintanceship,
but each one is really about building up a sense of trust between the individuals
involved. When trust fails or is shown to be lacking, we use powerful words to express
our disappointment. Someone who betrays our trust shatters our confidence
and destroys our faith in human nature. The end of trust leads to divorce and
estrangement for couples and to legal action and financial loss in business relations.

Our relationship with God at times resembles all sorts of human relationships, but I think that it is best thought of in terms of our most personal ones. We know God as a parent whose love for us is unconditional and totally dependable. But we need to get to know God as a lover whose love must be negotiated and won. Our development from childhood to adulthood involves exploring different kinds of relationships and discovering new forms of human trust. We do not remain children; we become friends, partners, members of communities. We must learn to be givers and sharers of love and, even harder, to become the objects and receivers of the love of others. Through all these human experiences we come to know as well what it means to be a child and partner of God.

Perhaps it is new and even shocking to you to think of God in this way. You are probably familiar with religious traditions where God is referred to as father or mother, but the picture of God as a lover feels too personal, too intense. Nevertheless, it is an image that is found at the heart of most traditions. In the Bible the Song of Songs is an erotic poem that likens the love of the individual for God to the passion two young lovers feel for one another.

> *"I am my beloved's, and he longs for me.*
> *Come beloved; come with me to the fields*
> *Let us rest in the village and go early to the vineyard.*
> *Let us see if the vine prospers, and the tender grape appears.*
> *There I will give you my love."*

Christian mystics, such as John of the Cross and Teresa of Avila, used the language of human love to express their ecstatic involvement with the divine. In Hinduism the god Krishna, celebrated as both child and youth, evokes both the love felt by parents, and especially mothers, for their children and the "sweet love" that draws lovers together. The message is that God is always there for us but from our perspective we each need to discover and grow in his love.

The women standing on the seashore of my home village in the past represent many kinds of love: the love of the parent, the sibling, and the spouse. They are experiencing a period of fear as they ponder the fate of their men during the storm. Their trust in God is being tested to the limit and they have nowhere else to place their hope. They count on him for protection and, as they do so, they must be recalling all the times when they have failed to live up to what they know are his standards and they must be making all sorts of promises for the future if only their men can be brought safely home.

The same kinds of thoughts go through all our minds as we try to wrestle with the many challenges and difficulties we encounter in our lives. Perhaps you have had a similar experience to the women fearing for the safety of their loved ones, or you have found yourself in such great danger that it seemed only some kind of divine intervention could save you. Your fears on the other hand may be the sort of thing that you would be ashamed or embarrassed to admit. They may seem so small and so

> *O God*
> *Take me by the hand, for I have*
> *nothing to present to You.*
> *Accept me, for I am unable to flee.*
> *Open a door, for You open all doors.*
> *Show the way for You make all ways.*
>
> PERSIAN SUFI PRAYER

trivial and yet they cause you a considerable amount of pain and anxiety. Most people have some personal horror or phobia to face, sometimes daily, that would mean nothing to anyone else. Practically everyone, I am sure, knows what it is like to suddenly feel afraid and yet not know what you are afraid of other than life itself.

At such moments it can be helpful to remember that the fear of God is the beginning of wisdom. Fear, for people who have found room for the spiritual in their lives, always carries the additional sense of awe and respect for the divine power that lies behind the natural world. If you are one of these people, and have begun to discover that that power is a personal God to whom we relate through the power of love, you will begin to see how the fear we experience when we are at the mercy of the elements is not very far removed from the wonder we feel before the majesty of nature. A prayer for protection is itself a kind of worship. When we beg God for help we are pleading with him to be our parent again. We become acutely aware of ourselves as the children we will always be. Do not be embarrassed to feel this way but allow your cry for help to be a song of praise to the one who made you, who has set you free to grow apart from him but is always ready to receive you back.

EXERCISE: EXPERIENCING THE GOD OF NATURE

• *Take the next opportunity that comes your way to experience the power of the elements. If you do not live within a reasonable distance of the countryside this may have to wait until the weekend or even until your next vacation. You do not need to find somewhere remote, just a place where nature feels more powerful than human effort. The seashore is an obvious place, as are the mountains or a thick forest. Try to be alone there, if only through putting a little distance between yourself and other people or by choosing a time of day or season when there are not so many people around. Choose a day when the weather is bad! Consider the words of the writer John Ruskin, who said that there is no such thing as bad weather, only different kinds of good weather. He was English so he probably still looked forward to a dry day, but if you lived in the desert you would plead for rain.*

• *Wrap up well. Take a thermos with a hot beverage and something to eat. Find some simple shelter, but try to feel what it is like to be at the mercy of the elements. Imagine people who are in precisely that situation: fishermen in small boats on a rough sea; travelers crossing a mountain pass on foot in a blizzard; the homeless on the wintry streets of a city. At a later time you might want to put images of such people in your Book to recall your meditation today.*

• *As you expose yourself to the elements, listen to the sound of the sea and the wind; observe the movement of the waves or the trees. Feel the strength of the power that is behind all this, and imagine yourself as a child helpless in every way and totally dependent on the protection of others.*

• *Now imagine someone you love exposed to the dangers of the forces surrounding you; see yourself struggling to help them and then embracing after the rescue.*

• *When you are home again, consider how thin the walls and windows of your house are and how close and vulnerable you remain always to the anger of the elements.*

God my father protect me
God my mother succor me
God my brother strive with me
God my sister comfort me
God my lover dance with me
God my friend accompany me
God my god find room for me.

A CELTIC PRAYER FOR
PROTECTION

In the name of God,
the most Merciful,
the most Compassionate.
Praise be to God,
the Lord of all worlds,
The infinitely Good,
the All-Merciful,
Master of the Day of Judgment,
You we worship,
and in You we seek help.
Guide us upon the
straight path,
The path of Your grace.

THE QUR'AN

Dear Lord, protect me:
The sea is so wide,
And my boat is so small.

A FISHERMAN'S PRAYER

6: asking for guidance

I am sure there have been many occasions in your life when you have had to make important decisions about the future. Which school should I apply to? Should I apply for that job? Am I prepared to go and live away from the place where I was brought up and from my family and friends in order to improve my opportunities and prospects? How did you make the decision? The classic way is to draw up a list of pros and cons and to see which column is the longer. Or perhaps you took advice from people older and wiser in the hope that their knowledge wasn't out of date and their idea of what was best for you came close to your own.

In many team sports, the kickoff is won by tossing a coin. Today we see this as just another form of choosing at random, but it was once a way of divining the right decision, in other words of identifying what God wanted in the circumstances. Divination was probably the principal way of making decisions in traditional societies and the reports of travelers and folklorists are full of all sorts of ingenious methods used by people to identify what they thought was the right way to act. Looking for patterns in tea leaves, coffee grounds, stones thrown on the ground, or rice vibrated on a drum were typical methods. People would also open a sacred book at random and choose a text without looking, then try to work out how it applied to the choice that had to be made.

Divination was also used to try to find out what was going to happen in the future. In Russia the days after Christmas were thought to be particularly good times to try to discover important information about what was to come. Young girls, for example, tried to discover what they could about their future husbands. All sorts of chance methods could provide information: placing a finger on a map to select a place name at random might suggest his name or location. Throwing a shoe through the door or seeing which way the next stranger passed by the window was supposed to signify the direction he would come from. The future husband would be rich if icicles on the house in winter were smooth, poor if they were not.

Although such techniques might appear today as superstitious and unscientific, we still read signs and depend on them to help us forecast the weather or the movements of the stock market—we just don't usually think we are identifying God's will when we do so, just simply what is most likely to happen.

Closer examination of divination traditions usually shows that an important preliminary to divination was to say a prayer. God was asked to reveal information through the throwing of dice or the drawing of straws. Professional diviners would employ complex rituals to call upon God to unveil the future. In old Tibet the State Oracle was consulted on all important decisions of government policy and by the judges of the high court. The Oracle would dress up in an elaborate costume and perform a wild dance that took him into a trance. Since people believed he was possessed by the divinity, they would ask him important questions. A steel mirror was held in front of his eyes, in which he could discern the future.

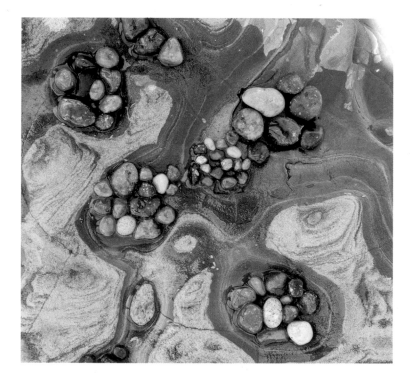

Practices such as this one belong to the specific cultures and belief systems in which they developed, but all of these practices share the belief that the God who knows the future is willing to share his knowledge with his faithful people. It is also clear that he does not usually do so in the form of clear and certain information; the message is always disguised or hidden in some way. Simply to let us know what was going to happen would present us with the kind of logical problems that intrigue science fiction writers and enthusiasts about time travel. If we could go  back in time, could we not change the future, which we have already experienced as the past? If we could go forward in time, could we not return with information that would allow us to ensure that the future we have already seen works out differently?

When we pray to God for guidance, we are not really asking him to show us the future. That would be too much to bear. Those Russian girls didn't really want exact information about their future husbands. That would have taken all the fun and romance away. What they wanted was some kind of clue to encourage them in their future relationships with eligible young men. Consulting an oracle was a way of expressing the divine dimension in human and worldly affairs, which cannot be planned for but that needs to be taken into account by religious people.

Most of us would probably be uneasy about the trivial nature of some of the old ways of divining the future, yet we might still feel that it is acceptable to ask God to give us signs of how we should act and behave. For example, today we do not think of dreams as visions of the future, but we understand that they can reveal to us hidden aspects of our personalities that might influence the way we act. Today we understand better the connections between the past and the future, and how the way we are brought up and the decisions we make can limit as well as increase our options for the future. Prayer for guidance, then, can begin with some reflection on our past. Maybe you have some kind of experience of counseling or therapy that has involved examining your personal history, but in any case most of us will recognize the importance such an examination has for us.

EXERCISE: EXPLORING YOUR ROOTS

• *In your Book draw your family tree as best you can. Include your parents, grandparents, uncles, and aunts. Think for a moment about each one of them. Even if you did not know them well you probably have some impression of their character or the reputation they had in the family. What aspects of them do you see in yourself or in your brothers and sisters? We are quick to identify physical characteristics, such as eye color, but personality traits also seem to get passed down the line. Even if you were brought up by parents or guardians other than your biological ones, you will probably have inherited patterns of behavior from them.*

• *When you have gone as far as you can with this exercise, you will probably be able to see how you are as much made up of other people's traits as you are of your own. How do you account for the particular ways in which you are you? If you have children of your own, how much of yourself do you see in them? How much do you see in them of your own parents? Generally speaking, we bring up our children either in a way very similar to the one in which we were brought up, or in a very different way. We either imitate our parents or we react against them.*

• *Try, in the future, to recognize the various people who have become part of you. Before you make an important decision, ask yourself who is really making this choice, to find out whether you are truly allowing yourself to act freely.*

When you are faced with uncertainty or with difficult decisions, remember that God wants what is best. This means that he wants you to choose how to act in the same way you would want for other people whom you love. He has given you freedom to choose but also plenty of clues about how to act appropriately. When you pray for guidance, you are praying that these clues will be clear and that you will not miss them, but most of all that you will be sensitive enough to recognize them in the first place. Prayer for guidance is therefore like all prayer— it is a prayer for personal transformation. We pray that we will change to conform more closely to God's will.

HOW TO MAKE A DECISION

• State clearly to yourself the matter you need to decide.

• Remember your determination to do God's will in the world, and your understanding that this is also what is best for you and for others.

• Be calm before the matter of decision.

• Try to be willing to accept whatever choice you make. Think of the way "the judge's decision is final" in a sporting event and how the players must accept that.

• Ask God to bring into your mind a sense of what you should decide and to make you feel drawn to that decision.

• Consider the advantages and disadvantages of each option.

• Pause and consider which choice seems to be coming through more strongly as the one you ought to make.

• If you were giving advice to a person for whom you wished the best, such as your own child, would you advise him or her to follow this course?

• Try to imagine looking back from the future, even perhaps from your deathbed, and ask yourself from that perspective how you would have wished you had acted.

• Imagine yourself standing before God and giving an account of your life. What decision would you wish you had made at the present time?

• Having made your decision, place yourself in prayer before God as someone who has freely and honestly made this choice, and ask for it to be accepted. Pray for some signs in the days and time to come that you have made the right decision. Accept that the signs may be a profound sense of assurance or just the absence of anything that might call your decision into question.

*The freshness of my eyes is
given to me in prayer.*

THE PROPHET MUHAMMAD

*Pray as if you see God, for if you do not see him,
he nevertheless sees you.*

MUSLIM HADITH

Love what God loves.

THE PROPHET MUHAMMAD

7: aids to prayer

After the revolution in Russia the new communist government launched a campaign against religion. One of the policies was to set up "antireligious" museums, which were filled with sacred books, objects, and pictures looted from closed churches and temples. One of the unforeseen consequences of this was that it gave people who had previously had experience of only one religion the opportunity to see and learn about the customs of others.

In today's multireligious societies we have the possibility of learning about other faiths in rather different circumstances. In this chapter I would like to look at some of the aids to prayer found in the many different religious traditions. Even if you do not decide to try any of these, it can still be helpful to have an awareness of them. Prayer is natural, but individual people differ, so there need to be different ways of prayer for different personalities. The more you are able to see the value for others of practices that might seem strange to you, the more you will be able to recognize what will be helpful to you.

PICTURES

We live in a visual culture. Just look at advertising, past and present. Where once you would have had a wordy poster going into all sorts of long-winded detail about the benefits of some product, today a film or picture "places" the product within some context that research has shown the target audience will find appealing.

Images have not been a part of worship in all religious traditions. Judaism, Islam, and some versions of Christianity have opposed the representation of the human form in particular. On the other hand, each of these traditions has found other ways of using beauty to raise the soul and inspire worship—for example, through calligraphy, architecture, or music.

In their private devotion many people find pictures helpful as a way of creating atmosphere or giving a focus for prayer. If you are praying for a loved one, it is natural to do so with their picture in front of you. Because you will want your prayer to go beyond your personal concerns to the well-being of the world and all its inhabitants, you might find it helpful to keep inspiring images taken from magazines in your personal Book. Turning the pages and spending a few moments on each image can become a helpful form of prayer.

PRAYER BEADS

The old English word *bead* actually means "prayer," and the use of beads in prayer has been popular in many of the great religious traditions.

In Catholic Christianity, people use a rosary to count their repetition of the prayer "Hail Mary" while they meditate on the mysteries of the life of Jesus. In Eastern Christianity, knotted ropes are used to count the saying of the Jesus Prayer ("Lord Jesus Christ, Son of God, have mercy on me a sinner"). In Islam, the beads can be used to "remember" the "beautiful names of God." In Hinduism, the telling of beads accompanies the mantras; in Buddhism it accompanies invocations of divinities or aspects of the Buddha.

The number of beads used in the different traditions varies considerably and is not all that important. You could probably make your own quite easily with a number that means something special to you.

Carry some beads around in your pocket or bag as a reminder of your commitment to a life of prayer whenever your fingers come across them. When you touch them, quickly repeat a few words of prayer that have meaning for you and that you have prepared for these moments. Your prayer could also be a single word, such as a divine name or the name of a person or issue you are praying for.

You could use beads more formally in your prayer life. You could make beads part of your routine in saying a given number of prayers or invocations at a particular time of day. See beads as an aid to concentration. It is not the number of prayers that matters, but the way in which they can be used to help you focus the mind for an instant on what really matters to you.

People who use beads find that they become less conscious of the meaning of the words they are reciting and more of the spiritual reality that can be met through them. The Tibetan word for telling the beads means to purr like a cat, suggesting how the saying of the prayers out loud can also be valuable, for example in generating a spiritual atmosphere in preparation for meditation or prayer.

PRAYER STONES

Stones have been used in religious traditions in a variety of ways throughout history. The most famous religious stone is part of the Ka'bah in Mecca. For Muslims this is the cornerstone of the earth, the place where the creation of the world began, and to which all Muslims are called to make a pilgrimage at least once in their lives.

The Jewish tradition includes placing a stone on a grave one has visited in memory of the dead. In other religious traditions, places of pilgrimage are often marked with stone cairns or piles of stone, each one being added by another pilgrim. The cairn itself then becomes a sacred marker to be treated with respect and passed or walked around in a ritual fashion.

In Tibet, prayer walls are found on hilltops, at bridges, and at the entrances to villages and temples. The act of placing a stone on them is accompanied by the exclamation "The gods are victorious" in thanksgiving for a safe arrival. Stones left in their natural setting might be marked with a prayer or mantra to uplift those passing by and to consecrate the natural landscape to the divine.

A small stone is one of the few pieces of the natural world that you can easily carry around with you and that is not going to make a mess or fall apart in your pocket. You could think of it as your personal link with nature. The feel of a smooth pebble or polished stone can be very soothing and, like the beads, can serve as a spur to prayer when your hands fall upon it.

THE WHEEL

The symbol of the wheel is found in many traditions, although the prayer wheel as a devotional device seems to have been confined to Tibetan Buddhism. In old Tibet the wheel was so closely associated with prayer and devotion that even the use of wheeled vehicles was thought of as sacrilegious and was avoided.

The prayer wheel is made up of a cylinder, within which a roll of paper or cloth inscribed with prayers or mantras is packed. Large prayer wheels may consist of large drums that are erected at temples and shrines and are designed to be turned by pilgrims or passers-by. Small wheels are mounted on a wooden handle with a pivot, and then a cord with a weight at the end is attached to help spin it. This is done with a twist of the wrist. The portable prayer wheel can be spun (always clockwise) while its owner is working or talking with others as an obvious sign of devotion and as an aid to concentration. The idea that the wheel activates the prayers without any effort or intention on the part of the devotee is probably a misunderstanding of this popular form of devotion.

Tibetan prayer wheels are now quite easily and widely available in the Western world. You might attract some unwelcome attention if you use a prayer wheel in public, but you might find it helpful during private devotional practices. There is no doubt that the gentle sound of the wheel turning is conducive to devotion. The sheer physicality of spinning the prayer wheel is so unlike anything in the traditional religious experience of Westerners that it could be valuable as an effective way of beginning a prayer period, helping you to make the transition from ordinary activity to spiritual activity.

The idea of the prayer wheel is not so remote from that of the *mezuzah*, the small box containing a prayer that is placed on the doorpost of Jewish homes and touched when entering. You might be able to think of other objects you could use as containers for prayers—the devotions can be "activated" by touching the object as you pass by or by making use of the object.

PHOTOGRAPHS AND PERSONAL ITEMS

I am sure you have sometimes come across old photographs, clippings, or letters
tucked inside a book when packing for a move or going through a family member's
affairs. The effect of suddenly being confronted with the past can be quite acute. You
could try to form the habit of uttering a short prayer on coming across such material
or being surprised in any circumstances. People often come out with a swear word on
such occasions. Try to be different!

Old photographs can be very powerful aids to prayer. They will often confront you with all sorts of memories and feelings that you might have been deliberately but unconsciously keeping out of mind. Treat their discovery as a gift from God and seize the opportunity to try to deal with the thoughts and emotions that they bring up for you.

When you have a quiet moment—as soon as possible after the discovery of the photographs—place them in front of you and pray that they might speak to you in the present. Does my success today derive from my poor treatment of others, or from selfish decisions, in the past? Is my lack of success today based on some unresolved resentment from the past? Is there any action I can take to at least symbolically redress the past? Offer your thoughts, memories, and feelings up to God and resolve to act differently in the future.

We often come across old school pictures and wonder what has become of so many young faces that were once our playmates. Pray for them, that whatever has become of them they have fulfillment in their lives.

Try to think seriously about how you would like to preserve old photographs and similar items. You could place them in context alongside others from the same period in an album, which might then help you find a sense of balance in the feelings they provoke. You may feel it is appropriate eventually to destroy some of them, but be careful that you are not doing so as an excuse not to deal with the issues they expose.

If you do decide to destroy something such as this, consider doing so by returning them to the elements through burning or burial, rather than by throwing them out with the trash. This is how many religious traditions often dispose of old prayer books or similar sacred items.

8: ritual prayer

Our ancestors lived in a magical universe. Their world was not governed so much by fixed natural laws as by spiritual forces that needed to be appeased and satisfied. How else could the unpredictable character of life be explained, the vagaries of health and the weather, sudden misfortune and death? God was ultimately responsible for all that happened, but he was far off and rarely seemed to intervene directly. For the most part it was local forces that were thought to be influential: the spirits of nature, of the river or the forest, and those that suddenly became powerful at particular seasons or times in the life of the individual or community. The people of the past dealt with these natural forces through a complex series of rituals that they believed could remove danger and ensure a positive outcome.

As long as the ritual was performed correctly, the desired effect was thought to be automatic. That is how magic is different from religion. Magic is only about knowing the right words and actions; religion is about having the right attitude and relationship with God. When we pray we do not expect that the mere recital of the words will bring something about. We do not know how or even whether God will respond to our prayers.

In most religious traditions ritual takes the form of reenacting important events in the history of that faith or of drawing attention to central teachings and beliefs. But the point is never just the giving of information. Religious ritual is believed to be effective in the same way as prayer is effective. Religious ritual is not a kind of magic, but a kind of prayer, a way of listening to God and bringing our concerns before him.

Think about the part religious ritual has played in your life and that of your family. What can you remember about weddings, funerals, and other special occasions you have attended? What do you know about the meaning of symbols such as the wedding ring or the funeral wreath? Perhaps you have been to ceremonies that were not officially religious but resembled sacred ceremonies, such as memorial days or

building dedications. What rituals did they involve and what was their purpose? Nowadays we tend to think of a ritual as being something out of the ordinary and detached from our everyday needs and concerns. Sometimes ritual behavior is even thought of as worrying, because it has no obvious practical purpose. In fact, the word *ritual* actually means "structure" and it is really the ordinary things you do regularly that are the rituals of your life.

You have only to think about life to see how it is full of ritual: the round of meals and journeys, going to and coming from work or school, watching television, visiting friends. Rather than thinking about adding ritual to our life of prayer, perhaps what we ought to be doing is turning our rituals into prayers.

EXERCISE: CONSIDERING YOUR RITUALS

• *Think of the things you do regularly each day, from getting up in the morning until you go to bed at night. Make a list of them in your Book. Don't worry about how trivial and mundane some of them seem; after all, they are probably the most vital to your health and well-being. Reflect on the list and try to think how each item can be turned into a prayer. Washing, for example, could easily make you think of your own desire to lead a purer life and of your concern for the health of the world's poor. Make a note of these prayers next to your routine and try tomorrow to offer these prayers as you move through the day.*

• *Meals and parties are very good examples of the importance of ritual in our lives. Having people to visit or going out to eat and drink are the most popular ways of celebrating friendships and social occasions, and every example is full of ritual behavior. Think of the way you set the table, the glasses and dishes you choose, the flowers and candles, the number and order of the courses. Consider how the same basic format can be transformed into a banquet or feast. The formality of meals reminds us of how rituals evolve naturally over time and always in a social context. They cannot just be invented by individuals. They derive their meaning from being shared and understood by others. A ritual that needs to be explained is not a ritual at all.*

Ritual meals are found in most religious traditions. There is a natural link between the food that maintains our bodies and the prayer that sustains our souls. Even when you are eating alone, try to observe a certain formality on occasions, giving thanks before and after eating and perhaps reflecting on the work of others that has gone into your meal. Even people who have still to discover their spiritual identities might be used to and appreciate some kind of dedication or blessing before eating, so offering one on social or public occasions can be your contribution toward bringing them closer to God. Such "graces" need not be explicitly religious if that is not appropriate or permitted, but they could include an invitation to consider the poor and hungry alongside thanks to those more immediately concerned with the preparation of the event.

Another important form of prayer that takes us out of ourselves to relate to others is blessing. How often do you say or hear the words "Bless you" or "God bless you?" Blessing may seem to have become little more than a wish or hope that things don't go too badly, whereas in reality it is one of the most fundamental and powerful forms of prayer.

Blessing is something we offer to the divine as part of our worship or prayer of adoration. In the Jewish and Christian traditions many prayers begin "Blessed are you, Lord God . . ." and go on to praise him for some aspect of his creation or activity in the world that is thought of as a blessing or divine gift. But blessing has also come to mean the way in which people, objects, or actions are transformed by being invested with sacred power. Whenever we use words such as *bless*, we are calling upon the divine to become present through a special act of power. We are doing far more than just saying "Have a nice day."

In many religious traditions some blessings have been reserved for particular individuals such as kings, priests, or heads of families, who are believed to have a special relationship with the divine and who can act as channels for sacred forces.

But since all true blessing begins with praise and depends upon the cooperation of the divine, there is no reason for ordinary blessings to be so restricted. In gatherings, though, it is usually a sign of respect to ask the senior person in attendance to give the blessing, and his or her experience or status will be regarded as adding to the efficacy of the prayer.

The giving of blessings is usually associated with particular gestures or rituals, such as touch or sprinkling with holy water. Generally, blessing is best associated with a change of posture, a moment of silence, and an action such as the raising of the right hand, and is completed with a word (*Amen*, meaning "so be it!") said by all.

There are many occasions when a blessing might be appropriate, more often perhaps than we are accustomed to thinking, and certainly more often than just after someone sneezes! A blessing at the start and completion of each new activity in your day can help create a climate of prayer in your daily life. The words you use may be very short and simple. They should begin with praise, for example: "Blessed are you God, source of Life. May the power of your love bless me and my colleagues as I begin my work today."

BLESSINGS

On waking

Blessed are you, light of the day!
Open my eyes to your glory and shine
on my path this day.

On rising

Blessed are you, rising sun!
Raise me from sleep to stand in your service.

On leaving home for the day

Blessed are you, guardian of the gate!
Guide me this day in the way of peace and love.

On returning home

Blessed are you, sanctifier of space and time!
Stay with me as evening falls and give your
servant rest.

On going to bed

Blessed are you, protector of your people!
Defend me from all danger and darkness.

EXERCISE: BLESSING AN OBJECT

Any object can be blessed, but usually we would reserve such a privilege for those intended for some kind of sacred use or for tasks associated with the continuing unfolding of the divine in the world. The tools of your trade—from spades to computers—are obvious examples, as are certain pieces of furniture in your home, such as the dining table and the bed. Items should be chosen because they have a function that is basic or essential to life and maybe also because you feel they may be vulnerable to misuse by yourself or others. Blessing should probably be reserved for a limited number of personal items rather than for everything we possess. Leisure items such as television sets and sporting equipment can probably remain in our lives unblessed!

Here is an exercise to identify those articles in your life calling to you for blessing.

• Pause for a moment and still your mind.

• Ask for the divine blessing upon your life and relationships in words such as "Blessed are you, lifegiver! May I share your sacred intention for the world in every aspect of my life."

• Think first of your home.

• Imagine entering the front door and moving slowly from room to room, trying to visualize what each room looks like.

• As your inner eye surveys your property, allow just one or two items to present themselves for your blessing. As always, never try to force anything in prayer; just let the items call out to you.

• At the end of your domestic exploration make a note of the items that wished to be affirmed.

• Give thanks for the blessings you have received in life and for the safety and privacy of your home. Pray for those who are homeless and lonely.

Repeat the exercise on another occasion for your office or workplace, remembering those who are unemployed or frustrated in their careers.

Blessed are You, the sacred origin of all things!
Thank You for allowing me to have the care of this . . .
Bless those who gave it its earthly form
and all who benefit from its use.
May it always be employed in Your service
and never be abused or allowed to serve evil ends.
May I share Your gift to me with all who revere You.

A PRAYER FOR BLESSING OBJECTS

(The object may be touched with blessed oil or water.)

Ritual is important because it reminds us that prayer should not only be a matter of words but should involve our bodies. In traditional societies the communication through the body, both in religious and everyday affairs, was far more common. People bowed and prostrated; they used hand gestures and facial expressions to express meaning; indeed these were often considered far more trustworthy than words. In the West, outside of churches, we see the remnants of such behavior in courtrooms and graduation ceremonies.

We cannot revive public ritual but there might be ways in which you can introduce bodily movements into your private devotion. You might think of sitting, standing, and bowing as ways of expressing different kinds of prayer apart from the words you use. You should persevere only with this if it comes naturally to you and does not feel artificial.

9: Remembering God's Name

"Whoever calls upon the name of the Lord will be saved." Joel 2.32

When I was at school we were always addressed by our surnames. I sat in the same classroom for years with boys whose first names I never knew. Even if someone did know your first name, they wouldn't use it unless they were invited to do so. In those days, first names were used only by close friends; today you are on first-name terms with people as soon as you have met them and it's family names that are hardly known. Living in these more relaxed times means that we have to find other ways of expressing our closeness to others. That we often do so by using nicknames or pet names shows how powerful we still feel names to be.

Today we are also uncomfortable with titles, and people brought up in the Christian tradition who were once accustomed to addressing God as "Lord" are more likely to speak to him directly as "God," as if that were his first name.

How then should we address God? What is his name?

In the Bible more than twenty names are actually used for God, and the one whose earthly name was Jesus is addressed in nearly two hundred different ways. In Islam the number of names for God is said to be unlimited, but it is said that those who memorize and understand the ninety-nine mentioned in the Qur'an and put their meaning into practice will enter Paradise. Guru Nanak, the founder of the Sikh religion, used names from both the Hindu and Muslim traditions for God as a way of suggesting that God did not belong to any one faith or people.

To the ancients a name was more than just a way of addressing or calling upon an individual. The name somehow expressed their essence; it went straight to the heart of the one so called. Choosing a name for a child was therefore a very important task and not just a matter of seeing what was currently fashionable.

In all religious traditions the names of saints, prophets, and great teachers have been popular. Individuals becoming religious professionals, such as priests or monks, usually change their given names to a "name in religion" or a "virtue" name to show their new status and identity.

When it comes to prayer it may be that you will feel most at ease using a divine name from your own culture or upbringing. These might equally have unhappy memories for you or not seem to properly express your actual experience of God.

In compiling this book I have found myself trying to avoid using too many gender-specific terms when I refer to God. I wanted to say "he or she," "himself or herself" all the time, but I found this very hard to do because I think I would rather call God "he" or "she" than seem undecided. I have to say that, probably because of my age and my upbringing, I usually do call God "he," but I hope you will feel free to change this if you wish.

Whichever pronouns you usually use when you address God, I think it is a good idea to try out the others as well. God cannot be pinned down by your choice of names or use of language, and using unfamiliar terms in prayer can be a good reminder of that. The level of concentration needed to avoid using specific gender terms in prayer can also be a helpful way of focusing and pacing your thoughts, as in the party game that most of us have played at some time where you have to avoid answering questions with "yes" or "no."

You may like to try something such as "Divine One" or "Holy One" as a form of direct address, or to simply and reverently use the personal pronoun "You," for example, "I come into Your presence" and "I place myself before You."

EXERCISE: REMEMBERING YOUR NAME

• *Think about your own name—the part your parents chose for you and the part you inherited from your family. Which part of your name do you use, or are you usually known by some other name altogether?*

• *Write your name down and look at the shape of the letters on the page.*

• *What do you know about the meaning of your names? Try to find out the historical meaning of your names. Does knowing the meaning affect the way you think about yourself?*

• *Do you know other people with one or more of your names?*

• *Are you happy with your name? Perhaps you would rather be called something else?*

• *Do you know why your parents chose those names for you? Were you named after someone in the family or someone they knew or admired? How does it feel to know this?*

• *Perhaps you have children and have had to decide on names for them. How did you go about that? Did you have disagreements with your partner? Why did you reject some names?*

• *Draw up a tree of family names from as far back as you can. Are there some names that are traditional to your family? Do some names seem hopelessly old-fashioned? Does your own name have a period feel to it that you think might allow people to guess your age today?*

• *Look at your name again on the paper in front of you. Does it now seem more or less your personal possession? Is that name really you?*

• *What if God had your name? What if God had your favorite name? Try calling on God using an ordinary human name such as these. Now call on God using a name from one of the traditions other than your own. Ask yourself how this makes you feel about God and about other people.*

In close human relationships, terms of endearment and private pet names are often substituted for proper ones, so in prayer itself you may discover a word that expresses your relationship with God. It's unlikely that this will be a name such as "Jack," but something along the lines of "Master" or "Teacher" could be a possibility.

"Remembering the name of God" is a spiritual practice known to several of the religious traditions. It doesn't mean reminding yourself in a casual sort of way that God exists and it would be a good idea to acknowledge the fact. Rather, it refers to a profound attempt on the part of the believer to place himself or herself in the presence of God. It is like the deep drawing in of breath we take before beginning some difficult task or attempting some athletic feat. All our experience and practice are going into this once-and-for-all moment. Everything is this second coming together, being remembered.

Think about your name for God, the name that best sums up for you everything you know and feel about the divine. Imagine the letters of the name, or of G-O-D, floating in the air freely and separately from one another. Slowly breathe in, very slowly at first, and then more powerfully. Imagine the letters being caught in your breath, positioning themselves to form the name, then being pulled closer by your breath until they finally unite as they enter your body.

This is an image of the goal of prayer that you can hold before you. Remembering God's name is a form of prayer for every stage of the journey.

In Eastern Christianity the best-known remembering prayer is the "Jesus Prayer," usually expressed as "Lord Jesus Christ, Son of God, have mercy on me." It has become familiar to many in the West through "The Way of the Pilgrim," the story of a poor and disabled Russian peasant who wanted to give himself completely to God in prayer. He was eventually advised to say the Jesus Prayer several thousand times a day and to increase the number and eventually double it, so that in the end he was no longer repeating the prayer. Instead, the prayer was saying itself in his mind and heart and even when he slept. As the Pilgrim wandered across the vast territory of Russia, his prayer transformed him and the people, animals, and nature he encountered.

The Pilgrim teaches us that remembering God's name is not something to do occasionally but as often as possible—and eventually, continually. In fact, all prayer has the same three stages, which have been called "oral," "mental," and "of the heart." We begin by saying our prayers, then we seek to develop a prayerful attitude and eventually to be transformed by prayer. Open yourself to this possibility and make it your desire to be so transformed. Repeat the name orally, slowly and clearly, several times, and try to continue hearing it even though your lips and tongue are no longer moving. Allow the name to banish all other thoughts from your head. Then imagine the name moving from your mind down to the center of your body, so that the name of God becomes the sound of your breath.

As you journey on, you will probably find that names and titles become less important than the sense of the divine presence invoked by your prayer.

The rivers in Paradise
They flow and say Allah, Allah.

YUNUS EMRE, FOURTEENTH-CENTURY MUSLIM POET

In the name of the One who taught the soul to pray,
Who illumined the mind with the light of the heart

PERSIAN SUFI PRAYER

Thy name is beautiful, thou art thyself beautiful.

YUNUS EMRE, FOURTEENTH-CENTURY MUSLIM POET

Hearing, remembering, and loving the name,
Immerses us in the sacred fount within.

GURU GRANTH SAHIB (SIKH SCRIPTURES)

10: praying in silence

"Men teach us how to talk; the gods teach us to keep silent," wrote the first-century Greek philosopher Plutarch. "He who speaks does not know; he who knows does not speak," says the Chinese proverb. All religious traditions have a special place for silence, because all religions are attempts to approach the reality beyond words that we call God.

But silence isn't the same thing as religion. You probably have your own experiences of silence and they may not always be good. You may associate silence with loneliness and lack of communication. The "silent system" was a nineteenth-century form of prison regime in which the inmates had no contact with their fellow prisoners and were supposed to spend their whole time reflecting on their misdeeds and the need for remorse. The only words they were allowed to hear were those of the prison chaplain exhorting them to reform. Ignoring someone remains a way of expressing dislike for them or disappointment at their behavior. Saying you are "not on speaking terms" says it all.

Perhaps these negative forms of silence come to mind first because we are no longer used to silence. Everywhere we go we seem to be bombarded with noise. We seem to have become frightened of quiet and need background music in shops and restaurants to keep our minds occupied. Personal stereo systems envelop us in a world of sound. It wasn't always like this. In traditional societies the sounds people heard came from nature or from their own activities. Farmers and craftsmen heard the sounds of their own labor and could often tell from them how well the tasks were being performed. The idea of blocking out these sounds with background music would have been considered undesirable and dangerous.

Think for a moment of how often in your day there are times of real silence. Late at night, if you are lucky, but then you are thinking about sleep. Early in the morning perhaps, but then you have to get up for work. When it is quiet do you make something of it or drown it out by turning on the radio or TV? Where would you go during the day to find silence?

There are many examples from the various religious traditions of seekers asking wise men and women for spiritual advice and being responded to with silence. The Buddha in particular answered many philosophers this way and so freed them from the illusion that they could possess the truth of things, for silence is closely associated with humility—the acceptance of your own limitations.

Human beings always want answers. They think that the world, reality, is some kind of question that, if only they can find the right "master" to ask, they can have explained for them. Imagine if this were so. Imagine coming before this wise teacher and being given the "secret" of the universe in a few words. What would you do then? Go and get a cup of coffee? Give your friends a call to share it with them? The world has a meaning, I am certain, but not one that can be reduced to a few words of explanation. Silence is the best response to those who think that it can.

Spiritual books dwell on the importance of silence, usually without pointing out that we are actually silent most of the time. Silence isn't some special mystical activity or state of which we have no experience. You have already thought about your day to ask how quiet it was. Now remember how silent you were. Even if you are in a job that involves a great deal of talking, the chances are that you are still silent for much of the time. Furthermore, speaking, finding the right words to say, is usually much harder than keeping silent. Not speaking might be a way of avoiding making mistakes, of keeping out of trouble or shunning gossip, but it does not demonstrate any particular commitment to taking responsibility or being involved in changing or improving things.

It's interesting that when we find silence in religious traditions, we actually discover something else. Most of us know that the people called Quakers or Friends worship in silence. The point of the silence, however, is that it allows people to speak when they feel moved or inspired to do so. The silence gives everyone the opportunity to speak without interruption or permission. By contrast, most other religious traditions have plenty of communal speaking and singing, and prepared addresses by authorized ministers, but the majority of "participants" remain individually silent.

I don't think it is so much silence itself that is important as what appears to be silence on the part of the person praying. I remember serving on a committee where everyone always seemed to have a lot to say and all sorts of ideas were argued around the table—everyone, that is, except for one individual who kept silent most of the time. When this person did speak, however, she invariably went to the heart of the matter, seeing through the other points of view, coming at the problem from a different angle, and giving a balanced response. Her suggestions usually became the committee's policy. The silent person was in fact a listening person, an attentive person, a person who did not necessarily have strong views of her own but who was prepared to consider the views of others critically and creatively and was dedicated to the work of the committee.

Silence, therefore, does not mean not talking. Silence can be a preparation for talking, a kind of container for thought and measured speaking. Closer attention to the teachings of the spiritual masters usually reveals that they give us plenty to do in the silence, not to block it out but to help us listen and develop attentiveness.

May the ears that have heard
Your word be deaf to clamor
and dispute;
May the tongues which have
sung Your praise be free from
deceit;
May the eyes which have seen
the tokens of Your love shine
with the light of hope.

ANCIENT INDIAN CHRISTIAN
PRAYER

We cannot speak about God and, as the philosopher Ludwig Wittgenstein said, if we cannot speak we must remain silent. But God speaks to us. So the starting point of all religion and spirituality is listening—keeping quiet so that we might hear the voice of God in our lives, in the lives of other people, in nature, and in the special places that God has revealed himself.

These special places are not always places in the geographical sense, but they could be. Reflect back on your life and try to recall a time and place when you felt particularly "in tune" with things, when you felt as if you were experiencing the divine. When I was a teenager I used to stay in a house situated on a clifftop overlooking the sea. There was one room where the view from the window seemed to meet the horizon, giving the impression that the vast expanse of water was immediately outside. I found myself drawn to this room and would often sit facing the window and the sea, experiencing, perhaps more in the allure than in the act, what I can describe only as a sense of the transcendent. It is many years since I have been to the house, but I still find myself taken there in my thoughts and dreams.

EXERCISE: LISTENING TO THE SILENCE

• *You may find it helpful to jot down in your Book places and times that come to mind, even if you do not yet associate them with special experiences. When you have a moment, think yourself back to them, try to immerse yourself in them by recounting as many details as you can of what they were like. Then just allow yourself to float freely among the details as you try to discover and experience again what struck you so long ago. This is the kind of listening-silence that distinguishes prayer from daydreaming. Prayer is an activity, not a kind of resignation. The person praying is like the "silent" committee member directing all her thoughts to the issue of the moment. The early Christian monks who cultivated silence, stillness, and solitude paradoxically used to compare their life of prayer to the feverish activity of bees around the hive.*

• *As you reflect on such special experiences, you may enjoy a sensation that has been likened to the "scales falling away from the eyes" or the "penny dropping," in which you suddenly and perhaps only momentarily catch a glimpse of the divine reality hidden behind them. Do not try to force such an insight, just be aware that it may be granted to you. Just stay with the event you recall and try to "listen" to it more closely.*

Some real geographical places are associated with this "in-breaking" of the divine. Usually they are sites of some kind of communal perception of the closeness of God where God or one of God's agents has appeared to people, or they are associated with important events in the history of a religious tradition. Such places become destinations for pilgrimages, but in my experience these can be rowdy occasions, opportunities for enthusiasts to meet up for a kind of moving convention! An out-of-season visit is often a better time for what I call a "listening pilgrimage."

Another kind of listening is that of spiritual reading. When we read sacred texts we don't just do so for information, or even inspiration, but because we believe that somehow God is addressing us directly through them. When we read sacred texts we attend to them in a special way: we "listen" to them.

EXERCISE: VISITING SPIRITUAL SITES

• *You are probably already aware of some location near you that either is or was considered a holy place. A little research at your local library or on the Internet will, I am sure, soon make you aware of one. Try to find out as much as you can about the place before visiting. Summarize what you have learned in your Book and reflect on it before setting off. The emphasis is on listening rather than pilgrimage, so do not worry too much about the journey, although a little effort—perhaps by using public rather than private transport—gets you in the mood.*

• *On arriving at the place take in the detail of its location and how the surroundings may have changed since its original identification. Walk around the site—the tradition is to do so clockwise—before going closer or entering it if it is a building or is located inside of one. Come to rest at the site and recall what you have discovered about it in your preparation for the day. Allow your thoughts to flow and float as you try to hear what the place has to say. Don't be tempted to try to force any experience; just reflect in the knowledge that this has been a place where, on some occasion and for some fellow seeker, time and eternity have met. Don't get too pious or sentimental either; buy a postcard or take a photo to afford yourself the opportunity to return to this holy place in your thoughts. The moment of epiphany, when all becomes clear, is just as likely to come to you in your remembering of the place as at the time of your actual visit.*

EXERCISE: EXPERIENCING SPIRITUAL TEXTS

• *Find a text that has meaning for you, because it is from your religious tradition or from one that speaks to you in some way. Start to read the words slowly, out loud if it feels right, allowing the sound and sense of each word to penetrate your body as well as your mind.*

• *Don't worry about "getting through" the text or even finishing a section or sentence. Just follow the words as far as they take you, giving them your full attention. The early Christian monks talked about "devouring" the words and chewing them through.*

• *Every so often a particular word or phrase will strike you, even though you might not be able to understand why. Stay with that word; see it floating before your inner eye and then becoming part of you.*

• *Stop when it feels right to do so—twenty minutes or so is about the right time for an exercise of this kind—and make a note in your Book of the words that have stood out for you and of any special feeling you experienced or "message" you received. Come back to these words later, treating them in prayer as you would the kind of special place we talked about earlier.*

Listening turns into silence almost without our noticing. As you become used to the ways of praying described in this chapter, you will find they bring about a new kind of attitude or approach to the world. By paying attention to special times, places, and texts you are training yourself to be more aware of every aspect of life as a vehicle of the divine. Listening for the sacred becomes second nature and is no longer an exercise we perform but a whole new attitude toward the world. The masters call this *attentiveness*. It is a kind of "active enlightenment" that meets incessant human questioning about the nature of things with silence, while giving full attention to the ways in which God is reflected in them.

Finally, remember the quiet committee member. Her silence eventually turned into powerful words. Spiritual silence is a way of engaging with the world, not of withdrawing from it.

11: SOLVING YOUR PROBLEMS WITH PRAYER

A seeker once asked a spiritual master to teach him prayer. The master said nothing and remained completely still, but flames seemed to surround his body for an instant. The seeker asked again. This time the master's body seemed to turn transparent and glow like light.

We usually think of prayer as something we do. How should I pray? How should I deal with the difficulties and distractions that make it hard for me to pray? What are the best methods of praying?

When the seeker asked the master for advice he was told nothing, but was shown that to pray is to be engulfed in flames or to be transformed into light. The fire and the light are not special spiritual tricks that the master has learned to perform; they are signs that his prayer has really brought him close to God, or rather that God has drawn near to him.

Although the human imagination is attracted to hidden mysteries and intrigued by the idea of esoteric spiritual teachings, there is really only one secret about prayer, although it's quite a big one. It is this: Although prayer seems like something we do, it is really something God does. Prayer is an incoming call on a telephone line laid by God and with God paying the bill! Now every time you see your telephone remember that God is calling and waiting for you to answer!

What we call *prayer* is really a response to God. The difficulties we have with prayer, those things that we think make prayer hard for us, are really the obstacles we place in the way of God's attempt to get through to us.

The biggest of these barriers, indeed probably the only really important one, is the way we lead our lives. Anyone who wants to take prayer seriously, who wants to embark on the spiritual path, needs to consider seriously the way in which they live.

The spiritual is not some kind of parallel world that you can occasionally visit and where you can have some kind of alternative identity that is unrelated to the kind of person you are normally. The world around you is the spiritual world, the one you live, work, eat, sleep, and die in.

It was the master's body that burned with fire and light, signaling that the presence of God is not just in our thoughts or in some special holy part of us, but in our whole being. We cannot therefore detach our way of life from our spiritual aspirations. Wrong behavior is what separates us from God, and this is the principal barrier to spiritual progress. All the religious traditions agree on this; there is none that says "Do what you will."

However, it is also a mistake to think that religion is principally a set of do's and don'ts, a complex list of regulations about how to behave in all sorts of circumstances. It is true that over the centuries the religious traditions have developed detailed codes of law and that these have sometimes achieved a rather exaggerated prominence in the lives of adherents, but all traditions also quote a sage or prophet who has reduced all law to one golden rule: Treat others as you would wish to be treated yourself.

The biggest obstacle to our growth in prayer is to be found in disordered personal relationships. Lack of love for others is the most disruptive factor in our own lives and in our spiritual quest. It is through others that we know God, and there is no way that we can grow toward God if we are growing away from other people. Monastic life, which has been present in most traditions in some form or other, is not, as is sometimes suggested, a retreat from the world but actually an intensification of human relationships in a school for prayer. You might not have spent any time in a monastery or religious community, but you may have been away to school or college and, if so, you will fully understand how the experience of living together can be described as a training in personal growth.

When you begin to pray, think about where you stand with other people. Have you got any outstanding quarrels or disagreements with friends or members of your family? The way we live today, the chances are that if you are in business you will have outstanding debts and ongoing rivalries and differences. Try to be realistic with yourself. God is not demanding perfection from you before he allows you to draw near to him. He is not standing there with a checklist of your faults, but is already drawing near to you, urging you and nudging you to try harder.

The word that seems to be used most often to describe difficulties with prayer is *distraction*. There always seems to be something you have to do before finding time for prayer, and then, when you do find the time, all sorts of things come into the mind to distract you. What you need to do is try to bring these possible distractions into the open before you begin—just as you might get all of your chores out of the way before you sit down to read or work on some project. You know when the dishes still need to be done and the dog needs its walk, but how can you guess what is going to disturb your prayer?

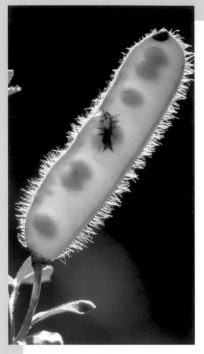

EXERCISE:
REMEMBERING YOURSELF`

A simple exercise recommended by many spiritual teachers can help us to see and deal with those barriers that get in the way of prayer. It consists of taking a little time to review your life, period by period, from back in your childhood up to the present moment.

• In your mind's eye, think about how your life naturally falls into different periods: childhood, adolescence, adulthood, for example. Think about how these periods themselves can be divided up into smaller units corresponding to different schools and colleges you went to, and then to various jobs you have had. Think again of how you have lived in several places, or how your home base has changed over the years. Think about your life in terms of the other people who have shared it closely with you: parents, grandparents, brothers and sisters, husbands or wives. Bring to mind your hobbies and interests, skills and commitments and think of the people involved with them.

• You will soon see how there are quite a few ways in which you can map out your life and a lot of different "angles" or "takes" you can have on it. There is you the grandchild, you the college kid, you the hockey player, you the homemaker. There are hundreds of you!

• You can do this quiet exercise while you do other tasks or to pass the time as you are traveling, or in any spare moment. At some point, though, you will probably want to set aside a little time to make a note of your many selves in your Book, and eventually you will need to settle down to meet them.

• *Spend a few minutes trying in your imagination and memory to be each of these selves again. Don't strain your thoughts; just think of each person you have been and allow them to speak to you. Maybe there are no words and you and your old self just smile at each other. Or maybe there is a tear for a time and relationship long lost.*

• *Although this may at first seem like it is going to be a huge task and last forever, in my experience the various steps of the exercise run into each other. As you think about a particular time in your life the feelings quickly return and the "issues" that still remain from that time re-present themselves. It's these issues that you are trying to identify and deal with, because these are the sources of distraction that stop you from praying. The things that come between you and your past, between you and other people are the same things that come between you and God.*

You may hardly need to do the exercise on the previous pages at all. Many people find that as soon as they begin to cast their minds over the past to meet their former selves, the issues that remain thrust themselves forward.

When I say "issues" I am thinking of any matter, big or small, that feels unresolved. Maybe you let someone down, took something that wasn't yours, or let someone else take the blame for something you did. Perhaps it is something more serious. You won't have forgotten the things that come between you and God and they won't let you forget them. You need to do something about them, which will obviously depend on what they are. If it is possible, you ought to try to right the wrongs, but be realistic about this and consider very closely the effect a return to the past will have on the other people involved.

If there is nothing you can do directly by way of making it up, or the issue is too general to be dealt with in this way, then some kind of symbolic act can be made to close the memory. The religious traditions offer many possibilities for this, such as a pilgrimage or fasting for more serious issues or for "lifetime" amends. A contemporary equivalent might be some voluntary work for a local charity.

Remember, the purpose of the exercise above is to help you to prepare for prayer, not to make you overly scrupulous about your past. The kind of issues it exposes are the sorts of things that prevent people from making a

> *O Great Spirit,*
> *Whose voice I hear in the winds,*
> *And whose breath gives life to all*
> *the world, hear me!*
> *I am small and weak.*
> *I need Your strength and wisdom.*
> *Let me walk in beauty, and make*
> *my eyes ever behold the red and*
> *purple sunset.*
> *Let me learn the lesson hidden in*
> *every leaf and rock.*
>
> FROM THE RED CLOUD
> NATIVE AMERICAN SCHOOL

> *Lord, be with us this day,*
> *Within us to purify us;*
> *Above us to draw us up;*
> *Beneath us to sustain us;*
> *Before us to lead us;*
> *Behind us to restrain us;*
> *Around us to protect us.*
>
> SAINT PATRICK

> *Lead, kindly light, amid the encircling gloom,*
> *Lead Thou me on!*
> *The night is dark, and I am far from home—*
> *Lead Thou me on!*
> *Keep Thou my feet: I do not ask to see*
> *The distant scene—one step enough for me.*
>
> JOHN HENRY NEWMAN

start by making them feel that they are not worthy or that it would be hypocritical to think that God was calling to them in prayer. It also identifies likely causes of distraction that may affect you at any time in your prayer. Simply being aware of these issues in advance can help you to deal with them when they arise.

Traditional guides often talk about our experiences during prayer in terms of the activities of angels and good and evil spirits. They do so to help us understand that when we pray we are opening ourselves up to realities outside of ourselves and beyond our control. In prayer we will undergo different kinds of feelings and thoughts and we need to have some way of understanding them and identifying what they mean.

Generally speaking, the "good spirit" will bring us comfort and perseverance in prayer, while the "bad spirit" will disturb and discourage us. However, there will be times when it could be said that the "bad spirit" brings peace and encouragement, because it would rather have you turned inward than working for justice in the world. And there might be times when it could be said the "good spirit" interferes with prayer in order to move you to speak out or take action.

> *My God, the soul You gave me is pure,*
> *You created it, You formed it,*
> *You breathed it into me,*
> *You preserve it within me.*
> *One day You will take it from me.*
> *I give You thanks, Lord of all souls.*
>
> ANCIENT JEWISH PRAYER

Distraction in prayer need not, therefore, be a bad thing. When you find your thoughts wandering while you are trying to pray, or particular images or ideas press themselves upon you during or outside of prayer, or even in your dreams, do not just try to push them away. All your thoughts and images are worthy of your attention, because they tell you something about yourself.

Stay with the distractions, but think of them as having a beginning, a middle, and an end. They appear, they speak to you, and they try to lead you somewhere. Observe them with your mind's eye in a detached sort of way. See where they are leading you. Don't struggle with them intellectually or emotionally, because they can often be quite powerful. Just see where they are taking you and consider whether you wish to follow.

If you have completed the exercise "Remembering yourself," (pages 100–101), you will recognize many of the distractions, and you will know where they are likely to lead. If it is somewhere you would not choose to go, use a short prayer such as a name of God or a word such as *love* or *mercy* to draw your attention back on course.

12: HOW DEEP CAN YOU GO?

Going deeper into prayer means going deeper into life, because prayer is not a way of escaping the world but of engaging with it. Only in the modern world have we come to think of religion and spirituality as distinct from the rest of life, almost as hobbies for those who have time on their hands. Our ancestors understood, and people in traditional societies knew, the dangers of neglecting the sacred.

We have to learn that, no matter how rich we are in possessions and material opportunities, we have only half a life if we disregard the spiritual. Furthermore, our wealth will inevitably involve the poverty of others. Even if you can see no direct connection between the way you are and the way others are, you know very well that you do not live in isolation from others. Your lifestyle is likely to have greater consequences for people thousands of miles away from you who produce the food you eat and manufacture the clothes you wear, than it does on your neighbors and those around you.

Prayer is God's language and it is a language all of us can speak. We cannot use it to keep secrets from God or from each other. To become fluent in this language we need to practice speaking it both to God and to one another. So prayer will always involve both what we think of as spiritual activities and the ways in which we make connections with other people.

Because we are so used to thinking of prayer as special and holy and as something that is very different from the ordinary ways in which we go about our lives, I think it is essential that we begin to go deeper by thinking about how we relate to others. In fact, I would go further than that and say that in order to go deeper in prayer, you need to identify some new way of encountering others.

The obvious way of doing this would be to join a prayer meeting, but I realize that what sounds as if it might be the first thing to do is not necessarily the easiest, particularly if you are coming from outside a certain religious tradition. Furthermore, you may end up finding yourself with people who are all looking inward and ignoring what is going on outside. What you really need is to find a way of being with people you don't normally meet. You might think about some kind of voluntary work, but I think just joining in a game or going to some kind of meeting might be better, because then you would be with people on equal terms. It might be a long time since you tried to get to know some new people, and since that is what you are trying to do with God, this is a good way of getting in some practice. Don't worry too much if you cannot find a handy group to link up with immediately; the important thing is to recognize the need to turn outward and to be on the lookout for opportunities.

Going deeper also means getting to know yourself a bit better. As you pray, God will frequently surprise you by suggesting new ways of coming to know him better. God knows you well and he will not demand from you what is beyond your abilities, but he also knows you are capable of more than you think and he wants you to stretch yourself to reach your potential.

Live, then, as someone who is looking out for God's call. Take seriously the invitations and possibilities that come your way. Look around for events and occasions in your area that might introduce you to new ways of knowing God. Be very careful, though; there is plenty of counterfeit religion around! What I am suggesting is an attitude of curiosity or generous detachment toward other people's ways of faith to discover what may be helpful to you personally. As a rule of thumb I would say groups that do not welcome visitors but demand immediate commitment are best avoided. Perhaps there is a long-established church nearby that you have never visited, or maybe a community new to your area has just established its temple. You'll probably find they are happy to welcome you to observe their worship from a quiet corner. Look out for groups that you know have very different styles to enrich your experience of devotion: the Friends or Quakers, for example, who make great use of silence in their worship, and Hindus and Orthodox Christians who employ elaborate ceremonial.

A retreat sounds like going backward but can be a very valuable way of deepening your prayer. Clergy and devout members of many religious traditions regularly spend time on retreat as a way of listening to God's call and reenergizing themselves.

A *retreat* is a time of withdrawal from normal activities to concentrate on spiritual matters. It is not just a time of rest and refreshment, for it can involve some demanding activity such as keeping silence, fasting or eating more simply, study, or manual labor. Retreat houses belonging to different traditions, particularly Buddhist and Christian, are now quite widespread and almost all will welcome visitors and give some basic guidance on how to make full use of the time there.

> *When you pray, go into your*
> *room, shut the door and*
> *pray to your Father who is*
> *in secret.*
>
> JESUS IN MATTHEW'S GOSPEL

In the Jewish religion, the Sabbath is seen as a kind of weekly retreat for everyone, commemorating the seventh day on which God rested after the six days of Creation. It is a day set apart for family, and for rest and study—a day on which, strictly, no creative work is undertaken. Christian and Buddhist retreats usually last for between three days and a week, but in both of these faiths there is also the tradition of withdrawing for considerably longer periods, even for a lifetime. For Christians the time that Jesus spent in the wilderness provides the authority for the retreat, and the Desert Fathers and Mothers, the ascetics of the early centuries of Christianity, are the model retreatants. Their sayings, which can be easily obtained, make excellent material for reflection during the inward journey.

In Buddhist countries young men from every kind of background will spend up to a year in a monastery as a kind of preparation for beginning to take on adult responsibilities, while in Tibet life is marked by a series of "withdrawals," in which religious observances replace secular pursuits. It is as natural to give over more time to prayer in the latter part of life as it is to devote the earlier part to preparing for a career or family.

Silence is the most important part of a retreat, although there are often opportunities to hear talks, participate in worship, and receive direct teaching from a leader. You can often join a group making a retreat around a particular theme or just spend the time on your own, in which case you might want to seek some guidance.

You could seek out someone to act as your spiritual director or "soul friend" at or through a retreat center. The idea of having a spiritual guide or companion is found in all the traditions as a way of helping those who wish to go deeper.

> *Go and sit in your room and*
> *your room will teach you*
> *everything.*
>
> ABBA MOSES

The idea is that someone who has a little more experience in treading the spiritual path can help you through any difficulties and provide you with material to move ahead. Spiritual friendship is a gift from God rather than a technique that is learned. No one really sets out to be a spiritual

Hate no one, blame no one, rebuke no one. God will give you peace and your meditation will be undisturbed.

ABBA PASTOR

director; it is more a case of discovering that people are coming to you for advice or help. A genuine guide will always be as willing to learn from his or her "students" as to teach them and will never try to force them to do things his or her way, but will help them discover how God is speaking to them personally. Especially in Zen Buddhism, it is often the case that a director will turn away individuals on many occasions as a way of testing their determination.

The hippies in the 1960s talked about dropping out of straight society as a way of rejecting materialist culture. When you go on retreat, or give over time for spiritual exercises, you too are dropping out but only as a way of preparing to drop right back in again with the hope of transforming your world. Genuine spiritual growth is always reflected in the way that you live, and so it always involves a willingness to change. Indeed, going deeper into prayer means just that, for no one is left unchanged by their encounter with God.

A brother stayed with a hermit and when he was leaving he said, "Forgive me for interrupting your prayer." The hermit replied, "My prayer is to welcome you and let you go in peace."

SAYINGS OF THE DESERT FATHERS

There was a monk who fasted completely every other day. A visitor came on a fast day and was entertained with a lavish meal. "Today I have fulfilled two commandments," the monk said. "I have received another with hospitality and I have set aside my own will."

SAYINGS OF THE DESERT FATHERS

A monk said to his guide, "Father, I have fasted, I have prayed, I have kept silence, I have tried to clean my heart of all thoughts of life outside my room. What shall I do now?" "Why not catch fire?" was the reply.

SAYINGS OF THE DESERT FATHERS

13: Developing a Daily Practice

*Wake up to a new joy today with
the new rays of the sun.
To a clean life which is good,
beautiful, and sparkling with love.
The wind of peace today
Carries the fragrance of the flowers
of eternity.*

RABINDRANATH TAGORE

Sometimes I am up late at night, because I am working late or have friends to visit, or just because there is something I want to watch on television. Sometimes I get up early because I have a plane to catch or I need a little more time to prepare for something special happening during the day. I rarely go to bed after 2 A.M., however, or get up much before 5 A.M. It occurs to me that in all my life I have rarely been up and about at 3 or 4 o'clock in the morning. Those two or three hours—we call them the "small" hours—are virtually unknown to most of us.

You might like to try on some occasion to visit the small hours. Go for a walk around your neighborhood just as it is becoming light, before the traffic has started and people set off for work. There are people who are active at this time: the emergency services, those involved in cleaning and preparing buildings for the arrival of the regular staff, news and postal workers, but it remains a curious sort of time when the familiar appears unfamiliar and the ordinary strange.

You can think of your life as being like a day. You are born at dawn, you grow in the morning, and reach maturity at noon. The afternoon represents your adult life, the evening your retirement, and then night falls and you find peace. The small hours are then like the time in the womb, or from the other perspective, your

*Spirit of God, make us open to
others in listening,
Generous to others in giving
And sensitive to others
in praying.*

FROM THE CHRISTIAN TRADITION

eternal rest. For those who believe in reincarnation the small hours have a particular meaning as standing for the time in between death and rebirth. Not surprisingly, one group of people who often make particular use of this time are those who live the monastic life. Monks and nuns of different traditions rise during the night to spend time in reading and prayer while the rest of the world sleeps.

*Prayer is better
than sleep!*

MUSLIM MORNING
PRAYER

The small hours are the time we all might give to God but cannot do so because of our need for sleep. Instead, we need to find moments of stillness and awareness in the midst of our busy and noisy days and we need to learn to find the eternal in our ordinary and familiar routine.

Our days have a rhythm that religious traditions have marked with prayer. Hindus pray three times a day—at dawn, midday, and dusk; Muslims pray five times—at dawn, noon, afternoon, sunset, and evening. Christians from the beginning prayed in the morning and the evening, and in monasteries up to seven times a day. In each case part of the purpose is to consecrate the entire day to God by stopping at regular intervals to offer praise.

Consider your own day. How does it naturally break down into sections? Rising and going to bed are the obvious terminal points. Setting out for work or school in the morning, returning in the afternoon, pausing for lunch and other breaks—each of these times brings a natural moment for offering prayer.

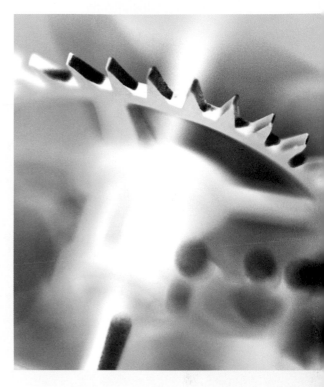

You could start by composing a simple prayer sentence appropriate for each time.

"I rise with the sun and pray for protection this day."
"I begin my work in your service."
"I rest in your care."
"I offer thanks for the day."

You could expand these prayers by seeing the day as a picture of your life, pausing for a moment in the morning to look to the years as well as the day ahead, and pausing at night to reflect on and give thanks for all that your life has been up until now. Or you could see the points in the day as standing for different ages, as I suggested earlier: childhood in the morning, youth at midday,

Take our minds and think through them, Take our hearts and set them on fire with love for You.

FROM THE CHRISTIAN TRADITION

and so on, and reflect in prayer on where or how you were or want to be at each time in your life. You could associate different times with different parts of your current life: with work, family relationships, colleagues, or more broadly with peace, the environment, and so on. Pause to reflect on and pray for each at a regular time. You will need to use your Book to record and schedule a prayer plan you have set for a week or for another period of time.

The value of this kind of prayer is that it is "objective." People say they don't pray because they cannot think of what to pray about, when they usually mean they can think of so many issues that they do not know where to start. Make a list of the things that concern you and that you want to pray about and give them a time of their own during your week. Dedicate a particular day to a concern and use each prayer moment to recall it and pray on it. Do not worry that this seems to sound rather mechanical and unspontaneous. By creating a structure you are giving yourself the opportunity to be flexible within it. You cannot improvise upon a musical instrument before you have learned how to play it!

Be careful, though, not to fill a busy day with busy prayers. Make sure that the time you take for prayer always includes a few moments of silence. You are the subject of God's prayer and he may want to communicate with you specifically in the midst of your busy life. Prayer is always a time for attention to what is going on around you, not indifference to it. There must be something wrong with praying for the rain forest because it is midday on a Wednesday, while some relationship in your workplace collapses or a colleague is in need.

Silence belongs to the substance of sanctity. In silence and hope are formed the strength of the saints.

THOMAS MERTON

Praying at set times is a valuable discipline, but we need also to understand that prayer is not just something we do now and then but rather a way of doing and being all the time. In other words, we need to be able to find the eternal in the ordinary.

Think again about your daily routine. It may involve some traveling that you could try to think of as a pilgrimage. Perhaps it involves some kind of routine that you could use meditatively to quietly recite a "list" prayer.

EXERCISE: PRAYING ON A JOURNEY

Most of us spend a lot of time traveling. We make regular journeys to work, to school, and to the supermarket, and we probably think of this as so much time wasted. But such routine journeys can be turned into a form of prayer.

• *Think about a journey you make regularly.*

• *In your mind recall the route you take and the places that you pass through on the way.*

• *Pay particular attention to places that strike you in some way because they interest you, maybe because their appearance attracts you or just because you like their names.*

• *Make a note of these places in your Book. Try to find about half a dozen of them, then sketch a little line map of your route with each of the places marked as bullets.*

• *In your prayer time reflect on why you have chosen these places. What are they saying to you? What images do they bring up?*

• *In your spare time try to find out a little more about places that intrigue you. When, for example, was that old church built? What does that odd place name mean?*

• *How do your personal associations with the place link to what you know about its real history or purpose?*

• *When you have an identity for each place, ask yourself what prayer it calls from you. A hospital obviously calls for prayer for the sick; a cemetery prayer for the dead; but a street or business name might call for prayer for a present or former friend or colleague. Use your imagination!*

• *When you make the same journey in the future, register these "prayer places" in your mind as you come to them and pass them and offer the appropriate prayer.*

EXERCISE: MAKING A LITANY OR "LIST" PRAYER

• *Think of the objects that you make use of (or even make) every day at work or school or in your own home.*

• *Make an association between each one and some intention for prayer. You could do this on the basis of what the item looks like or is used for. For example, a pen could stand for communication between friends, relatives, or parties in dispute; a safe or locked cupboard could represent the inner mystery at the heart of all things; a corridor could represent the route to illumination. The more way-out the association is, the easier it will be to remember!*

• *Alternatively you could make a list finding a subject for prayer for each letter of the alphabet in turn: awareness, blessing, communication, devotion, and so on. The list is your list so you can do what you want with it, mixing concepts with names and so on. As you carry out some routine task, run through the list in your head, pausing briefly on each item to turn the remembering memory into a prayer.*

You are Good, all Good, supreme Good,
You are love, You are wisdom.
You are humility, You are endurance.
You are rest, You are peace.
You are joy and gladness
You are justice and moderation.
You are all our riches and You suffice for us.
You are beauty, You are gentleness.
You are our protector,
You are guardian and defender.
You are courage, You are our haven and hope.
You are our faith, our great consolation.
You are our eternal life, great and wonderful God.

SAINT FRANCIS OF ASSISI

Lord, make me an instrument of Your peace.
Where there is hatred, let me sow love;
where there is injury, pardon;
where there is doubt, faith;
where there is despair, hope;
where there is darkness, light;
where there is sadness, joy.
O Divine Master, grant that I may not so much
seek to be consoled, as to console,
to be understood as to understand,
to be loved as to love.
For it is in giving that we receive,
It is in pardoning that we are pardoned,
and it is in dying that we are born to eternal life.

NINETEENTH-CENTURY FRENCH PRAYER

Further Reading

*The Mystic Vision: Daily Encounters with
the Divine*
Andrew Harvey. Published by Godsfield Press
(1996)

The Oxford Book of Prayer
George Appleton (Ed.) Published by Oxford
Paperbacks (2002)

*Learn to Pray: a practical guide to enriching
your life through prayer*
Marcus Braybrooke. Published by Duncan Baird
Publishers (2001)

Picture Acknowledgments

Corbis: pp: 6, 8, 12, 16/17, 20, 23, 25, 30, 32, 35, 38, 39, 63, 64, 66, 68, 95, 98, 99, 100, 102,
110, 113b, 119, 120/121, 123, 125. Image Bank: pp: 4, 5, 19, 28, 45, 46, 56, 61, 74, 79, 93, 108.
GettyOneStone: pp: 2, 9, 18, 31, 34, 43 ,60, 83, 84/85, 87, 88, 94, 112, 116, 117. NASA: p: 24.
Telegraph Colour Library: pp: 14, 15, 40, 47, 57, 65, 76, 86, 111.
Cover: Corbis/Stockmarket.

INDEX